Batsford's Walking Guides:
Thames Valley

Batsford's Walking Guides: Thames Valley

*Written and compiled
by Jilly MacLeod*

BATSFORD

First published in the United Kingdom in 2011 by
Batsford
10 Southcombe Street
London
W14 0RA
An imprint of Anova Books Company Ltd

ISBN 9781906388874

A CIP catalogue for this book is available from the
British Library.

20 19 18 17 16 15 14 13 12 11
10 9 8 7 6 5 4 3 2 1

Reproduction by Rival Colour Ltd, UK
Printed by 1010 Printing International Ltd, China

This book can be ordered direct from the publisher
at the website www.anovabooks.com, or try your
local bookshop.

Contents

Map of the Thames Valley

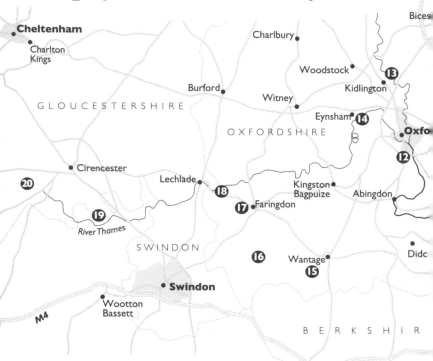

Bices

Cheltenham

Charlton
Kings

Charlbury

Woodstock

Kidlington

13

Burford

Witney

GLOUCESTERSHIRE

Eynsham **14**

OXFORDSHIRE

Oxfo

12

Cirencester

Lechlade

18

Kingston
Bagpuize

Abingdon

20

17 Faringdon

River Thames

19

SWINDON

16

Wantage

15

Didc

• **Swindon**

M4

Wootton
Bassett

BERKSHIR

Introduction

Rising in a field just north of the village of Kemble in Gloucestershire, the River Thames flows for over 340km (210 miles) through woods and water meadows, rolling hills, historic towns and picturesque villages to London and beyond. In its course it flows through three Areas of Outstanding Natural Beauty (AONBs) – and has a national trail – the Thames Path – running for almost its entire length, making it a magnet for walkers and other pleasure seekers.

The river began life some 170–140 millions years ago, at a time when most of southern England lay beneath the sea. The billions of tiny marine organisms laid down during this period gave rise to the limestone that forms the chalklands of the Thames Valley. As recently as 10,000 years ago, Britain was linked to mainland Europe and the Thames formed a tributary of the mighty Rhine – a link only severed when the waters rose once more and Britain was cut off from its neighbours. The name Thames possibly comes from the Sanskrit word 'tamas' meaning 'dark', or from a combination of the Roman 'tam' meaning 'wide' and 'isis' meaning 'water'.

Many walks in this book are based around the Thames Path, which largely runs along the towpath established towards the end of the 18th century to facilitate the flow of traffic along the river. Many landowners at this time refused permission for the towpath to be built on their land, which accounts for the fact that the path switches from one bank to the other along its course. For those seeking rural tranquility, walks upstream from Oxford are more remote, as the narrow river flows through water meadows grazed by sheep and very few towns

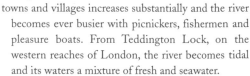

and villages. Downstream from Oxford, the number of towns and villages increases substantially and the river becomes ever busier with picnickers, fishermen and pleasure boats. From Teddington Lock, on the western reaches of London, the river becomes tidal and its waters a mixture of fresh and seawater.

A key attraction of walking in the Thames Valley lies in the rich wildlife: flowers such as marsh marigold, flag iris and purple loosestrife add colour in spring and summer and willow provides picturesque charm throughout the year. Birds include the mute swan, which gives rise to the annual ceremony of Swan Upping (see page 27), a variety of ducks including mallard, mandarin and wood ducks, plus Canada, Egyptian and bar-headed geese and other water birds such as the great-crested grebe, coot, moorhen, heron and kingfisher. Insects abound in summer, when dragonflies and damselflies can be seen flitting across the water, and common mammals include rabbits, stoats and weasels. The river otter is thankfully returning to the upper reaches but the water vole is still in sad decline.

THE WALKS

The walks featured in this book cover a wide range of different landscapes and points of interest: many follow the Thames itself, passing through well-known riverside towns such as Richmond (page 12), Eton (page 24), Henley-on-Thames (page 45) and Goring (page 52) along the way; others follow the river through more remote regions, such as Buscot (page 80) and the Cotswold Water Park (page 84) in Wiltshire. Away from the river itself, some walks take you alongside canals (page 60), across peaceful farmland visiting picturesque villages (pages 36, 49 and 68) and over rolling chalk downs (pages 40, 68 and 72), from where the views are spectacular, while others explore ancient woods (pages 20 and 40) and country house estates (pages 28 and 72). For those in search of wildlife, there are opportunities to visit nature reserves (pages 20 and 52), view red kites (page 40) and stroll through woodlands carpeted with bluebells in May (pages 20, 40 and 76). There are also special-interest walks, seeking out sites of historic importance such as Runnymede (where Magna Carta was signed, page 16), ancient hill forts (page 68) and chalk marks (page 72), or following in the footsteps of famous people, such as Prime Minister Benjamin Disraeli (page 28), designer William Morris (page 80) and members of the infamous Hell Fire Club (page 36).

Many of the routes are waymarked, making them easy to follow, and all are circular, with traditional country pubs along the way where you can stop off for some welcome refreshments. General advice on how to reach your starting point by car is provided, although it is always good to consider whether you can leave the car at home and take public transport instead (check www.traveline.org.uk before you go, especially as some bus services do not run on Sundays). Also provided are suggestions for local attractions that you may wish to combine with your walk, such as nearby gardens, country houses, model villages, railway museums and wildlife parks.

WALKING THE THAMES VALLEY

- Many of the walks may be damp and muddy after rain, so always wear suitable footwear: walking shoes or boots are advisable.
- If you are walking alone, let someone know where you are and when you expect to return.
- Consider taking a mobile phone with you, bearing in mind coverage can be patchy in rural areas.
- It is always advisable to take the relevant Ordnance Survey map with you on country walks, to supplement the maps provided.
- Some of the walks take you along small country lanes without pavements. Always walk facing oncoming traffic (except when approaching a right-hand bend when it is advisable to cross the road for a clear view), keep children and dogs under close control, and wear something light or brightly coloured when visibility is poor (at dusk, for example).
- Take special care of children beside water, particularly alongside canals where the sides can be steep and the water deep.
- Support the rural economy by spending your money in the local facilities, such as shops, cafés and pubs.
- While the author has taken every care to ensure the accuracy of this guidebook, changes to the walking routes may occur after publication.
- Public transport may also change over time, so if you are thinking of taking a bus to your destination, always check timetables and routes online or with local tourist information centres before setting out.

FOLLOW THE COUNTRYSIDE CODE

Here's how to respect, protect and enjoy the countryside:

- Always park sensibly, making sure that your vehicle is not blocking access to drives, fields and farm tracks.
- Leave gates as you find them or follow instructions on signs. If walking in a group, make sure the last person knows how to leave a gate.
- In fields where crops are growing, follow the paths wherever possible.
- Use gates, stiles or gaps in field boundaries when provided – climbing over walls, hedges and fences causes damage.
- Don't leave litter and leftover food – it not only spoils the beauty of the countryside but can be dangerous to wildlife and farm animals as well.
- Keep all dogs under strict control, particularly near livestock, and observe any requests to keep dogs on leads. (Remember, by law farmers are entitled to destroy a dog that injures or worries their animals.)
- Always clean up after your dog and get rid of the mess responsibly.
- Take special care not to damage, destroy or remove flowers, trees or even rocks: they provide homes and food for wildlife, and add to everybody's enjoyment of the countryside.
- Don't get too close to wild animals and farm animals as they can behave unpredictably.
- Be careful not to disturb ruins and historic sites.
- Be careful not to drop a match or smouldering cigarette at any time of the year, as this can cause fires.
- Get to know the signs and symbols used in the countryside. Visit the 'Finding your way' pages on Natural England's website for more information*.

* For full details of the countryside code, visit www.naturalengland.org.uk/ourwork/enjoying/countrysidecode

Leafy London Walk

RICHMOND, TWICKENHAM AND TEDDINGTON LOCK

*This classic riverside walk follows the Thames Path
upstream from the beautiful town of Richmond, along the north
bank through open parkland and leafy suburbs to Teddington Lock,
where you cross over the footbridge for the return journey. As you
pass through picturesque meadows, with their tide-washed willows
and rich birdsong, you might almost imagine yourself to be in
a remote country estate. Along the way, you have the opportunity
to visit some historic Thames-side houses, from the Jacobean
splendour of Ham House to the Palladian elegance
of Marble Hill House.*

DISTANCE:	9.5km (6 miles) (circular)
TIME:	Allow 3–4 hours
LEVEL:	Easy
START/PARKING:	The Square, Richmond (TW9 1BP). Car parking available on Paradise Road, in Old Deer Park off Twickenham Road (A316) or at the station. OS grid reference TQ180749 (OS Explorer map 161)
GETTING THERE:	*By car:* From central London, take A4/M4 to junction 1, turning off on to A205 South Circular Road; fork right on to A307 into Richmond *By public transport:* Underground to Richmond Station
REFRESHMENTS:	Many cafés and pubs in Richmond, White Swan, Twickenham, or Tide End Cottage in Teddington
LOCAL ATTRACTIONS:	Ham House (National Trust); Marble Hill House (English Heritage); Strawberry Hill

DIRECTIONS

1. From the Square, walk down George Street, then turn left into Hill Street and right over Richmond Bridge. Turn left at the end of the bridge and take the Thames Path down to the riverside. Turn right and follow the path upstream as it leaves the built-up area behind.

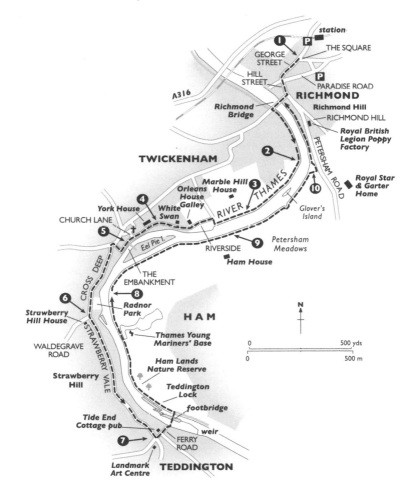

2. As the river makes a broad sweep round to the right, look across to the opposite bank where you can see Richmond's Royal Star & Garter Home rising majestically from the trees. Designed to house disabled ex-servicemen and women, the home gets its name from the old Star & Garter Hotel where it was established in 1916. A little further along the route the river broadens out and you are afforded glorious views of Petersham Meadows at the foot of Richmond Hill.

3. Beyond Glover's Island you soon pass the entrance to Marble Hill House, the Palladian villa built for Henrietta Howard, mistress of George II. Go under the footbridge into Riverside and the Orleans House Gallery, Richmond Borough's principle art gallery, which has an Octagon Room designed by leading Georgian architect James Gibbs. Carry on along the lane towards Twickenham, past the charming houses clustered round The White Swan.

4. Pass under another footbridge and take a peek at the riverside gardens belonging to 17th-century York House (owned by Twickenham Council). Pause on entering the Embankment to visit St Mary's Church where Alexander Pope lies buried in the nave (although his skull is said to have been exhumed). You may also choose to make a brief detour to visit the little shops in Church Lane.

5. Walk down the tree-lined Embankment, with its footbridge to Eel Pie Island, bearing right into Wharf Lane, then sharp left into Cross Deep. At the traffic lights, turn left into Radnor Park, where the seats are well placed to enjoy the view. The war memorial here is specially sited so that it can be seen from Richmond's Royal Star & Garter Home, along a sight line down Ham House Avenue, which links Twickenham visually with Richmond Hill.

6. Continue to follow the Thames Path out of the gardens and left along Strawberry Vale. Strawberry Hill, a recently restored 18-century Gothic castle created by Horace Walpole, is tucked away here down Waldegrave Road – well worth a visit if you have the time. Strawberry Vale eventually becomes Twickenham Road, which in turn becomes Manor Road. At the crossroads with Teddington High Street, you can take a brief detour to visit the Landmark Art Centre in the cathedral-like church to your right.

7. Turn left down Ferry Road, past The Tide End Cottage pub, and continue over Teddington Lock footbridge to the south bank, enjoying a bird's-eye view of the lock and weir along the way. Now turn left on to the broad and gravely Thames Path, which runs above the sloping river bank through Ham Lands Nature Reserve, created on gravel pits in-filled with rubble from London's wartime bomb sites. Ignoring the paths that disappear inland among the trees, follow the path alongside the river, crossing the entrance of the huge lagoon that forms the Thames Young Mariners' Base.

8. Further on, you will see the Gothic summerhouse of Radnor Park come into view on the far bank, followed by Eel Pie Island and the jetty of the Richmond Boat Yacht Club. Ahead, the skyline seems suddenly taken up by the commanding Royal Star & Garter Home. Before long, the path opens out to the entrance of Ham House, an outstanding survival of a 17th-century Stuart house, which in its heyday was a hotbed of court intrigue.

9. Soon you pass the stage for the ferry to Marble Hill House on your left and, beyond that, Ham Polo Club on your right, which welcomes match spectators. Five minutes further on affords you the classic view of cattle grazing in Petersham Meadows, with the steep rise to Richmond Hill beyond. Shortly, the Thames Path skirts the meadows wall to enter Riverside Park. Ahead of you lies Richmond Bridge, but if you look back along the river you'll find there's not a single building in sight.

10. Walk on through the park, turning left on to Petersham Road for timed tours of the Royal British Legion Poppy Factory, which turns out 32 million poppies and 80,000 wreaths every year. Keep beside the river as it passes the Richmond Canoe Club, restaurants, cafés and bars, walking under the arch of the Richmond Bridge and into the sociable buzz of historic Richmond waterfront. From here you can return to your starting point via Water Lane.

Courtesy of the Natural England/Thames Path National Trail/Transport for London.
For more information and similar walks see www.nationaltrail.co.uk/thamespath and
www.tfl.gov.uk/tfl/gettingaround/walkfinder

Memorials, Monuments and Magna Carta

COOPER'S HILL AND RUNNYMEDE

*Set beside the Thames, just 4.5km (3 miles) south-east
of Windsor, this short walk takes you through an area steeped
in English history. From the heights of Cooper's Hill, overlooking
the valley, you make your way down to the water meadows at
Runnymede, passing the John F Kennedy Memorial on your way.
Further on lies the Magna Carta Monument, commemorating
King John's historic sealing of Magna Carta in 1215. From here
you follow the Thames Path for a while before heading back across
the meadows to the foot of Cooper's Hill. A brief climb brings you
back to your starting point, by way of the Air Forces Memorial.*

DISTANCE:	6.5km (4 miles) (circular)
TIME:	Allow 2–2½ hours
LEVEL:	Moderate (with one steep climb)
START/PARKING:	Cooper's Hill Lane car park, Englefield Green (TW20 0LB). OS grid reference SU995719 (OS Explorer map 160)
GETTING THERE:	*By car:* Take A30 to Englefield Green (between Egham and Sunningdale); turn on to A328 then right on to Cooper's Hill Lane, bearing right to car park *By public transport:* Train to Slough or Egham, then take Sough/Heathrow Airport bus no. 71 to Englefield Green at Cooper's Hill Lane
REFRESHMENTS:	Refreshment chalet at Runnymede Pleasure Ground
LOCAL ATTRACTIONS:	The Royal Landscape, Great Windsor Park; Thorpe Park

DIRECTIONS

1. Turn left out of the car park into Cooper's Hill Lane and walk for 400m (440yd) past the red brick walls surrounding what was once the site of Brunel University Runnymede Campus to reach Priest Hill at the end. Turn right and walk on the narrow grass verge down the hill. After a couple of hundred metres take the first turning on the right, by the footpath sign, through the gate into Oak Lane.

2. Follow the track as it winds past the old university grounds down the hill to the John F Kennedy Memorial. This simple memorial bears the inscription: 'This acre of English Ground was given to the United States of America by the people of Britain in memory of John F Kennedy, President of the United States of America 1961–1963'. Take the flight of cobblestone steps just on the right-hand side of the memorial and carry on down the hill and into Runnymede Meadows.

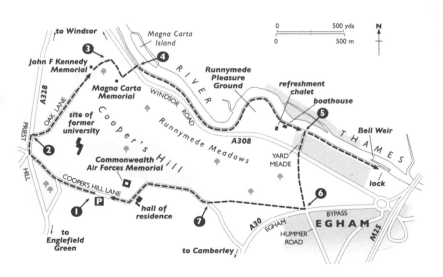

3. Turn right through the gate and walk along the field boundary until you reach the Magna Carta Memorial on the right-hand side. This temple-like structure is set in an enclosure and was erected in 1957 by the American Bar Association to commemorate the sealing of the charter in 1215. The central plinth bears the following inscription: 'Dedicated in 1957 by the American Bar Association, as a tribute to the Magna Carta: symbol of freedom under law'. With your back to the memorial, walk towards the Windsor Road, crossing the road with care to reach the bank of the River Thames. Magna Carta Island lies directly ahead.

4. Turn to your right and walk downstream along the river bank heading towards Egham. After a short time you pass a public footpath sign directing you into Runnymede Pleasure Ground. This area of open space is very popular during the summer season, when the river bank may be full of people quietly fishing and the field behind populated by families, picnicking and enjoying the open air. Pass the former bathing pavilion and children's paddling pool, making a short detour to the refreshment chalet and public toilets if necessary, rejoining the towpath by the Wraysbury Skiff and Punting Club boathouse. Continue along the towpath.

5. On reaching Yard Mead you have a choice. You can either turn right down the road to emerge on to the main Windsor Road (to begin your return journey) or continue further along the towpath to Bell Weir to watch the myriad boats passing through the lock. If you decide to walk this latter stretch, retrace your steps back to Yard Mead to continue the route. On reaching the Windsor Road cross the road with care and follow Public Footpath No. 12(E), which leads towards Egham Bypass at this point. Head along this tarmac path towards Hummer Road, with the Tower of Egham Church visible ahead.

6. On reaching the wooden footpath signs, turn to the right down Public Footpath No. 15(E) until you come to a hedge. Follow alongside this until you reach a gate and stile. Pass through these and walk along the bank of the stream to two concrete stepping stones. Turn left uphill, crossing the stile and turning right into Cooper's Hill Lane.

7. Climb to the top of the hill, bearing left at the lookout. Pass Kingswood Hall of Residence (part of Royal Holloway College) on your left-hand side and the Commonwealth Air Forces Memorial on your right. The memorial was designed by Sir Edward Maufe and consists of a shrine enclosed by cloisters. Her Majesty Queen Elizabeth II unveiled the memorial in 1953 as a fitting tribute to the 20,000 servicemen and women of the Air Forces who died during World War II and have no known graves. For a commanding view of the River Thames and its surrounding area climb the stairs to the roof area. Rejoin the road and turn right to head towards Cooper's Hill car park where the walk began.

Courtesy of Runnymede Borough Council. One of a series
of Runnymede Rambles available at www.runnymede.gov.uk

SIGN OR RESIGN!

Under pressure from his barons who sought to limit his power and make him subject to the law, King John sealed Magna Carta – or the Great Charter of Liberties – on 15th June 1215. Comprising 63 clauses, the charter covered a wide range of subjects, from the right to trial for all free men to uniformity of weights and measures, and later became an important model for countries such as the USA when drafting their own constitutions. It is not known for sure where the historic event took place, whether on the water meadows at Runnymede or on Magna Carta Island. Runnymede, however, is believed to have been a special meeting place long before 1215, and may take its name from the Anglo-Saxon term 'runieg', meaning regular meeting, and 'mede', meaning meadow.

Tranquil Woodland Walk

HEDGERLEY, EGYPT WOODS AND CHURCH WOOD

Set only a few miles west of London in a richly wooded area, among rolling hills and surrounded by a patchwork of fields, this tranquil walk leads you through sun-dappled woodlands where bluebells carpet the floor in spring and birdsong fills the air. Starting out from Hedgerley Hill, the route takes you in a double loop through Kemsly Wood and on into Egypt Woods, part of Burnham Beeches and a Site of Special Scientific Interest thanks to its complex of habitats and rich wildlife, including 56 resident species of bird. From here you loop back through Hedgerley to explore the area to the east of the village, where Church Wood provides the perfect place for more birdwatching.

DISTANCE:	5.5km (3½ miles) (double loop)
TIME:	Allow 1½–2 hours
LEVEL:	Easy
START/PARKING:	Bus stop on Hedgerley Hill, south of Cottage Park Road, Hedgerley (SL2 3RW). On-street parking available on Hedgerley Hill. (A small parking area is also available at Collinswood Road end of Harehatch Lane, should you choose to start at a different point.) OS grid reference SU968866 (OS Explorer map 172)
GETTING THERE:	*By car:* Turn off M40 at junction 2 on to A355 towards Slough, turning right on to Parish Lane and left on to Hedgerley Hill *By public transport:* Train to Slough, then Slough/High Wycombe bus no. 74 to Harehatch Lane (on A355), joining walk at direction 5
REFRESHMENTS:	The White Horse, Hedgerley
LOCAL ATTRACTIONS:	Bekonscot Model Village; John Milton's Cottage

DIRECTIONS

1. From the bus stop, follow the waymarked path through Kemsly Wood (called Footpath Wood on some maps), keeping to the right-hand path by the wooden hut. Kemsly Wood is mixed woodland with mainly oak, beech and birch, and varied ground cover dominated by ivy, bluebells, bracken or nettles. When you reach Parish Lane turn right and, taking great care, walk along the road to the crossroads.

2. Continue straight ahead at the crossroads and after approximately 300m (330yd) take the footpath to the left through Ponds Wood. Carefully cross Collinswood Road (A355) and follow the path opposite through the next block of woodland to Egypt Lane.

3. Cross the lane and follow the estate road into Egypt Woods. These woods take their name from the old gypsy encampments that used to be set up here, and are the northern part of a larger area of woodland known as Burnham Beeches. These woodlands are a Site of Special Scientific Interest, containing many rare habitats and, in the south, unique ancient pollarded beeches. Egypt Woods are used for shooting from October to February, so it is important that you keep to the waymarked paths, avoiding the timber extraction rides leading off and keeping your dog under close control, preferably on its lead.

4. At the junction of the tracks turn sharp right, back along the woodland boundary, and follow the path back into the woods. Scots pine, larch, woodsage and honeysuckle add to the rich variety of woodland smells here, especially during the summer months.

5. Cross the A355 once more, taking the estate road down to Pennlands Farm. This was the site of a brickworks until 1936. The kiln produced 20,000 bricks per firing. Old clay pits are still visible to the north of the track. The farm has many 18th-century barns including one on settle stones. The stones were designed to keep out rats and mice, and to allow air underneath, keeping the grain dry. Continue along the track to the crossroads.

6. Carefully cross the road into Kiln Lane and head towards Hedgerley village. The names Kiln Lane and Kiln Wood (to your right) show the importance of brickmaking in Hedgerley's history. At the T-junction, turn left through the village. Judge Jeffreys (1644–1690) of 'Bloody Assizes' fame was Hedgerley's most famous resident, ending his days in the Tower of London following a spectacular career that saw him Chancellor at the age of 40.

7. After about 200m (220yd) take the path to the right up past the church. The present church of St Mary the Virgin is the third on the site and was built in 1852. The previous churches were of less solid construction and suffered the effects of springs rising under the site. Follow the bridleway uphill, bearing right at the top of the incline towards Hedgerley Green.

8. When you reach Wapseys Lane, turn right towards the M40. During the construction of the motorway two Roman pottery kilns were discovered, showing that Hedgerley clay was valued as long ago as the 2nd century AD. After 200m (220yd) turn right on to the public bridleway. Banks and ditches visible along the path were dug to define old woodland boundaries. A stand of semi-mature hornbeam can be seen on either side.

A Wood for All Seasons

Owned by the RSPB, Church Wood is a rewarding place for a quiet stroll at any time of the year. In spring the woodland floor is carpeted in bluebells and the air is filled with the birdsong of blue, great and coal tits, greenfinches, chaffinches, blackbirds and song thrushes. While the birds are busy feeding their young, look out for  butterflies such as the white and red admiral, marbled white, comma and peacock in the summer months. In autumn, when the trees are awash with colour, visitors such as fieldfare and redwing can be found, while fungi such as fly agaric, dog stinkhorn and King Alfred's cakes flourish. Listen out for mistle and song thrushes in winter, and keep an eye out for buzzards and kites circling overhead.

9. At the junction of the paths turn right, heading west back towards Hedgerley. There may be cattle or sheep in these fields, so please ensure you keep your dog on its lead. The path takes you alongside Church Wood, an RSPB reserve comprising typical mixed woodland with mainly native species. Two trails have been marked out in the woods giving the quiet walker the opportunity to spot many native woodland birds, including the brightly coloured jay, buzzards and kites (see special feature, above).

10. Upon reaching Hedgerley, turn left to retrace your steps through the village, then turn right back along Kiln Lane.

11. Halfway along, take the waymarked footpath to the left through Kiln Wood, following the waymarkers to Kemsly Wood and eventually back to your starting point on Hedgerley Hill. The path through Kiln Wood is steep and can be slippery during wet weather. An alternative route is to follow Kiln Lane to its end and turn left up Andrew Hill Lane – look out for the old brick kilns in gardens near the bottom of the hill. At the bend in the road, bear left into Kemsly Wood, then left again to take you back to Hedgerley Hill.

Courtesy of Buckinghamshire County Council. For more information go to www.buckscc.gov.uk/bcc/row/walks.page

Eton Riverside Ramble

ETON AND ETON WICK

This walk starts out at Windsor Bridge, beneath the towering edifice of Windsor Castle and close by Eton College Boat House, from where the colourful flotilla of Swan Uppers sets out each year. From here you cross the Thames and join up with the Thames Path, following the river upstream as it meanders through fields and meadows. The route takes you beneath Isambard Kingdom Brunel's famous Bowstring Bridge – the oldest wrought-iron bridge still in regular use – past Windsor Race Course and on to the village of Eton Wick, where you can stop for refreshments before making your way back along a tree-lined stream inappropriately known as Common Ditch.

DISTANCE:	5.5km (3½ miles) (circular)
TIME:	Allow 1½–2 hours
LEVEL:	Easy
START/PARKING:	Windsor Bridge (SL4 1PX). Parking is available in any of Windsor's main car parks. OS grid reference SU967772 (OS Explorer map 160)
GETTING THERE:	*By car:* Take M4 to junction 6, turning south on to A355; continue on to A332 and turn left at second roundabout into Clarence Road *By public transport:* Train to Windsor
REFRESHMENTS:	Plenty of cafés and pubs in Windsor or The Greyhound in Eton Wick
LOCAL ATTRACTIONS:	Windsor Castle; Legoland

DIRECTIONS

1. Starting from the south side of Windsor Bridge, cross the River Thames walking towards Eton. Take the first turning on the left and pass between The Waterman's Arms public house and Eton College Boat House on to The Brocas – a wide open meadow named after a local family. The meadow was later acquired by Eton College in the 15th century. Local farmers can still exercise their Lammas Rights by grazing their cattle here in August. Follow the Thames Path alongside the river to the railway bridge, pausing to look back at the splendid view of Windsor Castle, which is the largest inhabited castle in Europe.

2. The railway bridge and viaduct carry the branch line of the former Great Western Railway from Slough to Windsor. The main line, which opened

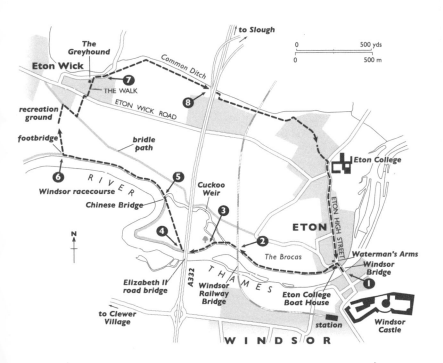

in 1848, made a wide detour around Eton because the College authorities feared the boys would be led into temptation by its presence. The bridge itself is a fine example of a wrought iron 'bowstring' bridge with a single span of 51m (167ft), engineered by Isambard Kingdom Brunel to avoid the need for piers in the river, which would have interfered with navigation. Continue under the railway bridge and alongside the river, crossing two small bridges over the backwaters.

3. The path now leads you through a small wood which, despite the well-used paths running through it, still contains a wide variety of birds, butterflies and plants. Bats have been seen around the edge of the wood and over the river. Continue under the Elizabeth II road bridge, built in 1960 to carry the relief road from Slough and the M4 to the west of Windsor.

4. Shortly after the bridge bear right, taking the main path across a large meadow. The river ahead of you flows in a dogleg that has been known by generations of oarsmen as Upper and Lower Hope (if you prefer, you can follow the riverside path). At the start of the meadow, look back to see the spire of St Andrew's Church in Clewer Village on the opposite bank. The path and the river come together again at the Chinese Bridge (rebuilt in 1994), so called because of its wooden structure. Under the bridge the backwater flows into Cuckoo Weir where the Swan Lifeline Headquarters and Treatment Centre – committed to the rescue and care of sick and injured mute swans – is situated. Cuckoo Weir was originally the site of a mill, owned by Burnham Abbey until the dissolution of the monasteries. Further down the backwater lie the remains of 'The Sandy', a bathing place that was closed shortly after World War II following an outbreak of infantile paralysis (polio).

5. Leaving the Chinese Bridge carry on along the path beside the river, from where you can see the Windsor Racecourse buildings on the opposite bank. Next look for a seat at the back of which is a plaque marking the bathing place known as 'Athens', once used by Eton College boys who were not in the habit of wearing bathing costumes.

6. As you get towards the end of the reach turn right immediately before the small concrete footbridge and continue past the recreation ground up to the bungalows at Eton Wick. Turn right here and walk along the bridle path for 30m (33yd), then turn left on to a narrow path that heads towards the main road. Watching out for traffic, cross Eton Wick Road diagonally right and go down The Walk, stopping at The Greyhound pub for refreshments if the fancy takes you.

7. Turn right at the T-junction at the end of The Walk and follow the road round to the left. Before the road passes over the Common Ditch cross over the stile on the right and follow the path, keeping close to the stream on your left while you look out for wild flowers along the bank. Continue along the path through the pasture until you reach the relief road overhead.

8. Pass under the road and carry on beneath the marvelous 100-arch brick viaduct, also designed by Brunel and one of the longest such brick viaducts in the world. At the end of the field, in the right-hand corner, go through the gate that leads on to a small road. Turn right, passing the College buildings with the dome of the College Library straight ahead. Turn right again on to Eton High Street from where you can return to your starting point at Windsor Bridge.

Courtesy of the Royal Borough of Windsor and Maidenhead. For more information go to www.rbwm.gov.uk

SWAN UPPING

Swan Upping is an annual census of the swan population along certain stretches of the Thames, which takes place between Sunbury and Abingdon during the third week of July under the direction of the Queen's Swan Marker. The ceremony dates back to the 12th century when all mute swans were owned by the Crown and swan was an important part of the menu at royal feasts and banquets. By the 15th century the Vintner's and Dyer's Companies had been extended ownership rights and to this day their representatives accompany the Queen's own Swan Uppers – resplendent in their scarlet uniforms – as they set off in a small flotilla of traditional Thames rowing skiffs to ring the birds.

In the Steps of Disraeli

HUGHENDEN MANOR

This fascinating walk takes you on an exploration of Hughenden Manor Estate, once owned by Victorian Prime Minister Benjamin Disraeli who made this his country seat from 1848 until his death in 1881. The 6.5km (4 miles) route takes you across a rich and varied landscape, over gently rolling hills and through colourful beechwoods, rich pastures and elegant parkland. Along the way you will have the chance to explore the Disraeli Monument, a pet cemetery and the church where Disraeli and various family members lie buried. Afterwards, you have the option of visiting the manor house which has a wealth of personal memorabilia on display (charges apply).

DISTANCE:	6.5km (4 miles) (circular)
TIME:	Allow 2–2½ hours
LEVEL:	Moderate
START/PARKING:	Hughenden Manor ticket office (National Trust: HP14 4LA). OS grid reference SU866955 (OS Explorer map 172). Parking available
GETTING THERE:	*By car:* Turn off A40 in High Wycombe on to A4128, heading north towards Kingshill; turn left and follow drive 0.5km (⅓ mile) through parkland
	By public transport: Take train to High Wycombe, then bus no. 300 towards Aylesbury, alighting at entrance to drive
REFRESHMENTS:	Restaurant in stable yard near car park
LOCAL ATTRACTIONS:	Hughenden Manor; Odds Farm Park

DIRECTIONS

1. From Hughenden Manor ticket office walk up the stairs and turn right towards the woodland car park, passing the orchard on your left. Follow the red arrows for the duration of the walk.

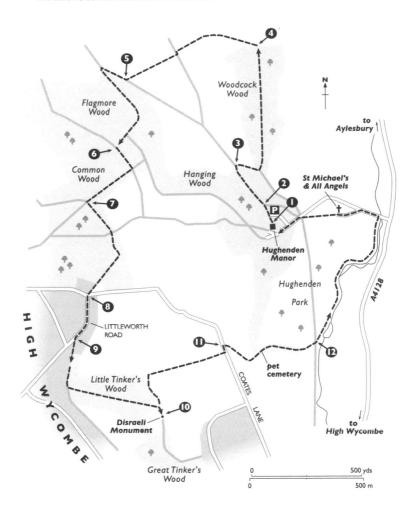

2. At the crossroad near the notice board take the left track – the Coffin Path – into the woods, keeping the car park to your right. The Coffin Path is an ancient road that was used to transport the dead from Naphill to Hughenden church in medieval times. If you look closely you may see where the flint surface has been ground down by iron wheels. The road almost certainly marks the edge of a Saxon field boundary.

3. Once through the wood, turn right along the edge of the field and carry on into Woodcock Wood. Turn left at the crossroad and continue straight through the woods, going over another crossroad where the path falls steeply and rises again. You may notice various pits along the course of this walk, particularly here in Woodcock Wood and in Flagmore Wood. These range in size from small saw pits – approximately 3 x 5m (9 x 6½ft) – to large flint, clay or marl extraction pits, which can be up to 10m (33ft) across. The material from these larger pits was used as building material and also as a way of adjusting acidity levels in local farm soils.

4. At the edge of the wood, go through the metal gate into the field and bear diagonally left towards the next gate. Once through the gate, follow the path straight ahead along the field boundary, keeping the hedge to your right. Cross over the large flint track and continue through the next field, this time keeping the hedge to your left.

5. Follow the path as it bends to the right along the woodland boundary and turn left though the gate into Flagmore Wood. Bear right where the path forks and go straight over the next crossing point down the slope. Then bear right at the large fork and continue straight down until you reach a track at the bottom of the hill.

6. Turn left on to the track. After a short distance the track ends opposite a gate; turn right before the gate and up the slope, following this path uphill until it reaches another path running alongside a boundary ditch.

7. Turn left, keeping the ditch to the right. Go down the slope and straight up the next slope, following the path until it exits the woods, passing between two fences. Take care as you approach a main road.

8. Cross the road and follow the path opposite alongside Littleworth Road until you come to a public footpath on the left at house number 78, opposite a brick and flint cottage.

9. Cross at the tarmac drive and go through the gate. Follow the path behind some houses, bearing left at the first fork and right at the second fork at the edge of Little Tinker's Wood. Go through the woods and out through the gate, heading across the field to the Disraeli Monument.

10. Built to commemorate Disraeli's father, Isaac D'Israeli, this Grade II* listed monument was erected in 1862 as a surprise gift for Disraeli from his wife, Mary Anne. Leave the field by the same gate through which you entered and turn right, following the path to the bottom of the hill. Turn right at the bottom through a gate and follow the field boundary to Coates Lane.

11. Cross the road and turn left then immediately right on to a track and through a metal gate. Follow the track and go through a gate into the park. Look out for the pet cemetery at the edge of the park, where Disraeli's heir and nephew, Coningsby Disraeli, erected five tombstones in memory of his beloved dogs – you will find the graves on the far side of a metal fence. Continue through the park, bearing right towards the stream.

12. When you reach the stream, turn left, keeping the stream on your right until you get to the main drive. Turn left along the drive and follow the path round the chapel of St Michael's and All Angels – Disraeli's final resting place. When Disraeli died on 19th April 1881, Queen Victoria was so upset by the death of her favourite Prime Minister and friend that she sent two wreaths of primroses to the funeral, bearing the note: 'His favourite flowers: from Osborne: a tribute of affectionate regard from Queen Victoria.' To finish your walk, continue towards the manor until you reach the stable yard and your starting point.

Courtesy of The National Trust. For similar walks go to
www.nationaltrust.org.uk/walks

Poets, Spooks and Spinneys

MARLOW CIRCULAR WALK

*This delightful walk begins at the riverside town of Marlow –
once home to poets Shelley and TS Eliot, and described by Jerome
K Jerome in* Three Men in a Boat *as 'one of the pleasantest river
centres I know of'. From here the route takes you along the Thames
– 'where the river is at its best' – and past what is said to be the
most haunted house in Berkshire. You then head through the
meadows into a series of spinneys and woods, finally emerging
into open farmland on the return path to Marlow. The route
is easy to follow, being waymarked with yellow arrows at
every gate or major change of direction.*

DISTANCE:	9.5km (6 miles) (circular) or shorter route of 4.5km (3 miles)
TIME:	Allow 3–4 hours (shorter route: 1½–2 hours)
LEVEL:	Easy
START/PARKING:	The War Memorial on Marlow High Street. Parking available off Pound Lane (SL7 2AE). OS grid reference SU850863 (OS Explorer map 172)
GETTING THERE:	*By car:* Turn off M40 at junction 4 on to A404; turn right on to A4155 to Marlow *By public transport:* By train to Marlow Station
REFRESHMENTS:	The Three Horseshoes, Marlow, or The King's Head, Little Marlow
LOCAL ATTRACTIONS:	Cliveden (National Trust)

DIRECTIONS

1. Follow the footpath across Higginson Park to the riverbank and head upstream on the towpath, away from the town. The wet meadows on this side of the river support abundant wild flowers such as meadowsweet and lady's smock. The damp conditions also suit the alder trees that line the riverbank along this stretch.

2. Across the river stands Bisham Abbey, a manor house dating from about 1260, which Henry VIII gave to his fourth wife, Anne of Cleves, as part of their divorce settlement, and where Elizabeth I was later held captive. The abbey is reputedly haunted by the ghost of one-time owner Lady Holby who still walks the corridors, having murdered her son for blotting his copybook (see special feature, page 35). Continue along the towpath.

3. For now, ignore the footpath leading off to the right and continue on to Temple Lock, originally built in 1773 to replace the earlier flash lock. Flash locks consisted of only a single gate and were very wasteful of water – it was

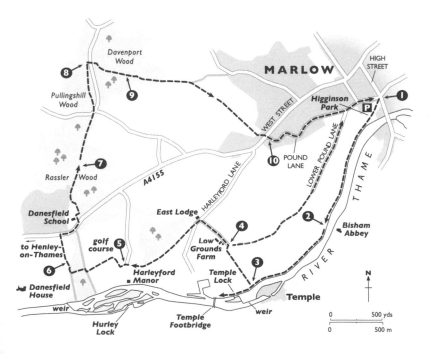

said that after the flash lock had been opened the river would drain for almost 24 hours, making it possible to walk across dry-footed. Unusually, when the new lock was built in 1890, the old one was left in place alongside it. Today, you can still cross the river dry-footed by walking over the award-winning Temple Footbridge (opened in 1989), which lies a further 200m (220yd) upstream, connecting Buckinghamshire and Berkshire. Now retrace your steps back to point 3 on the map and take the footpath off to the left, heading north away from the river towards Low Grounds Farm.

4. Upon reaching the farm you can either turn right and take the path back to Marlow for a shorter walk, or follow the route round to the left, past the farm and on towards East Lodge. Turn left at the lodge and head for Harleyford Manor (built in 1755 for Sir William Clayton).

5. Cross the manor driveway and follow the waymarked route around the edge of the golf course, bearing right and left as necessary. At the far corner of the golf course, head into the spinney as marked, bearing right on the far side.

6. As you emerge into the open, look across to your left: beyond the trees lies Danesfield House estate, once the base of RAF Medmenham, a photographic intelligence unit that was to imagery intelligence what Bletchley Park was to signals intelligence during World War II. Follow the path north and cross the busy A4155 with care. Turn right and walk along the verge, turning left on to footpath that takes you past Danesfield School and up into Rassler Wood.

7. Rassler Wood is an area of mixed woodland with a canopy dominated by beech, horse chestnut and cherry, and an under storey of birch and holly. The ground flora includes bracken, brambles and an abundance of bluebells in the spring. Continue along the path, crossing a minor road, and on through Pullingshill Wood until you reach another road.

8. At the road, the footpath crosses from the east to the west side of the adjacent banks. Banks such as these were used to define the limits of ownership of woodland. In this case the banks have also been adopted as part of the parish boundary between Great Marlow and Medmenham, indicating that they probably date back to Saxon times and beyond. Cross the road and head east towards Marlow.

9. Continue to follow the waymarked route through Davenport Wood, which is home to a variety of birds including green and greater-spotted woodpeckers, nuthatches, jays, great tits, blue tits and coal tits, all of which may be spotted by the quiet walker. Upon leaving the wood, follow the path through the dry valley, bearing right where the path forks.

10. When you reach the A4155, cross the road with care and continue along Pound Lane back into Marlow town centre. The town is well worth a look around. A popular place of residence since the 18th century, there are some fine examples of Georgian architecture to be found. Notable residents included Percy and Mary Shelley, who lived for a year at 104 West Street, where Percy composed *The Revolt of Islam* and Mary finished *Frankenstein*. A hundred years later TS Eliot took up residence at 31 West Street, to escape the bombing of London during World War I.

Courtesy of Buckinghamshire County Council. For more information go to www.buckscc.gov.uk/bcc/row/walks.page

THE LEGEND OF LADY HOLBY

When the monks were evicted from Bisham Abbey in 1536, so the story goes, the abbot put a curse on the sons of all future inhabitants. One such was young William Holby, youngest son of Lady Elizabeth Holby, whose ambition for her children led her to educate them herself. One day, up in the tower room, after William had blotted his copybook for the umpteenth time, his mother became so incensed that she beat him around the head until he bled and tied him to a chair. She then set off on horseback to abate her anger, but upon receiving an invitation to court from Queen Elizabeth I, she forgot all else and headed straight off. Returning several days later and realizing her son was not there to greet her, she dashed to the tower room only to find him dead. To this day her ghost is said to haunt the abbey, moaning and frantically trying to wash her son's blood from her hands.

Of Monks and Meadows

HAMBLEDEN AND MEDMENHAM

*Starting out from Mill End, situated on the north bank of
the Thames between Henley and Marlow, this lovely walk takes
you along the Hamble valley to the pretty village of Hambleden,
birthplace of Lord Cardigan (of Light Brigade fame). From here
you pass through fields and woodlands to Medmenham village,
once the site of the notorious 'Monks of Medmenham', also
known as the Hell Fire Club. The delightful return journey
follows the towpath upstream along the Thames, with an
optional extension to view the weir across the river
and the beautiful Hambleden Mill.*

DISTANCE:	9km (5½ miles) (circular)
TIME:	Allow 2½– 3½ hours
LEVEL:	Moderate (with several stiles and steep slopes)
START/PARKING:	Kissing gate at junction, just north of Mill End village. Park in Mill End car park (RG9 6TL). OS grid reference SU785854 (OS Explorer map 172)
GETTING THERE:	*By car:* Turn off M40 at junction 4 on to A404; turn right on to A4155 and right again at Mill End, heading towards Hambleden *By public transport:* By train to Marlow Station, then catch bus no. 800/850 towards Henley-on-Thames, getting off at Mill End, Hambleden
REFRESHMENTS:	The Stag and Huntsman, Hambleden, or Ye Olde Dog and Badger, Medmenham
LOCAL ATTRACTIONS:	The Hell-Fire Caves at West Wycombe

DIRECTIONS

1. From Mill End car park, turn right and walk down the road until you reach a lane off to the left. (If you are travelling by bus, from the bus stop walk up through the village to the lane on your right, just past Yewden Lodge.) Go through the kissing gate on your left and follow the footpath alongside Hamble Brook to Hambleden village.

2. Bear right into Hambleden and walk past The Stag and Huntsman public house, stopping off for refreshment if the fancy takes you. Hambleden is one of the prettiest villages in Buckinghamshire, with its cobbled pavements, village pump and charming old cottages built out of flint and brick. The church has parts that date back to the 14th century, though it was much restored and altered in Victorian times. Some fine oak panelling inside is reputed to be the bed head

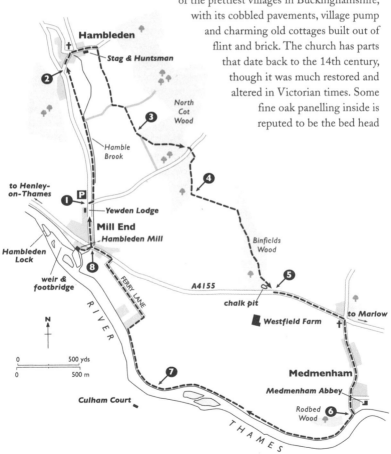

belonging to Cardinal Wolsey! Continue straight out of the village along a drive (signed Private Road) and turn right at the fork, along the rough track. Walk back along the valley, turning left at the next fork, and then right, until you reach the edge of North Cot Wood.

3. These woods are dominated by beech trees, which grow well in the chalky, well-drained soils; the trees would have been planted to supply the Chiltern furniture industry based at High Wycombe. The timber is hard and easily worked, stained or bent into curves, making it ideal for chair-making. Fork left where the path splits and carry on through the woodland until you reach the road for Mill End. Cross the road and continue following the path round the edge of the woods.

4. Turn left, following the path between two fields, and carry on through Binfields Wood to reach the main road near Westfield Farm. The old chalk pit on your right, at the south-east corner of the woods, was quarried at the end of the 19th century. The chalk here is harder than many of the sediments known as chalk and was used as a building material for the nearby mansion, Danesfield House, as well as for a few houses in Medmenham.

5. Turn left along the road and then right at the church to take you into Medmenham. Just beyond the village once stood the Cistercian Abbey of St Mary, abandoned during the dissolution of the monasteries. The abbey masonry was later used to build an Elizabethan manor house, which, having become derelict by the 18th century, was refashioned in 1755 by Sir Francis Dashwood. He added a 'ruined' folly tower and a cloister arcade, transforming Medmenham Abbey into a suitable meeting place for his notorious club – the Knights of St Francis, better known as the Medmenham Monks or Hell Fire Club (see special feature, opposite).

6. Walk on to the river and turn right to follow the towpath upstream. The small wet woodland to your right, Rodbed Wood, is a Site of Special Scientific

Interest. The trees here are mainly willow, alder and ash, beneath which grows an interesting selection of wet-loving plants, including yellow flag, marsh marigold and summer snowflake, known locally as the Loddon Lily.

7. Across the river at this point lies Culham Court, a square Georgian mansion built in 1770 with terraced gardens leading down to the river. George III once stayed here and was greatly impressed by the hot rolls carried by a relay of horses from his favourite baker in London. Continue along the path until you reach a group of houses. Turn right, away from the river, and then follow Ferry Lane around to the main road. Turn left on to the A4155 then right to take you back to your starting point.

8. Alternatively, take a short detour and turn left just beyond the Mill End turning. This takes you back down to the river's edge from where you can view the weir across the Thames and the beautiful Hambleden Mill, now converted into flats. A series of bridges over the weir and across Hambleden Lock on the far side are usually open to the public and are well worth crossing to get a real appreciation of the power of the water at this point.

Courtesy of Buckinghamshire County Council. For more
information go to www.buckscc.gov.uk/bcc/row/walks.page

THE MONKS OF MEDMENHAM

Sir John Dashwood, known as 'the worst Chancellor who ever lived', had founded the Knights of St Francis in 1746, comprising men of fashion and rank that included one ex-Prime Minister, several cabinet ministers and the First Lord of the Admiralty. By 1750 they were meeting in Medmenham Abbey, suitably attired and now calling themselves the Medmenham Monks. Rumours soon abounded of 'nuns' cavorting in the gardens, orgies and Satanic rituals, and critics started calling them the Hell Fire Club, based on a notorious club of the same name from the 1720s. Their downfall came when radical politician John Wilkes released a baboon dressed as the devil into their midst, causing members to start praying and confessing their sins. Things were never quite the same again!

Red Kite Walk

STUDLEY GREEN AND RADNAGE

*Situated in the Chilterns in the Thames Valley Region,
less than 13km (8 miles) north of the Thames itself, this
fantastic walk provides the perfect opportunity for watching
one of England's most spectacular birds – the red kite (see special
feature, page 43). Starting out in Stanley Green, the route takes
you through beautiful valleys, ancient woods and rolling farmland,
providing panoramic views along the way plus the chance to stop
off in a traditional country pub. Your return journey from
Radnage takes you through Bottom Wood, an ancient
wood managed as a nature reserve, which is awash
with bluebells in early May.*

DISTANCE:	9km (5½ miles) (circular)
TIME:	Allow 2½–3½ hours
LEVEL:	Moderate (many stiles and several steep uphill slopes)
START/PARKING:	Garden centre on A40 in Studley Green (HP14 3XL). OS grid reference SU783953 (OS Explorer map 171). Park in garden centre (closes 5pm)
GETTING THERE:	*By car:* Leave M40 at junction 5 on to A40 towards West Wycombe, reaching Studley Green after about 6.5km (4 miles) *By public transport:* Train to High Wycombe, then catch bus no. 2A or 40 towards Stokenchurch
REFRESHMENTS:	The Three Horseshoes, Bennett End
LOCAL ATTRACTIONS:	West Wycombe Park (National Trust)

DIRECTIONS

1. From the garden centre, cross the A40 with care and turn left towards Stokenchurch. After about 100m (110yd) turn right on to the footpath and head diagonally right across the field towards the corner of the wood. Follow

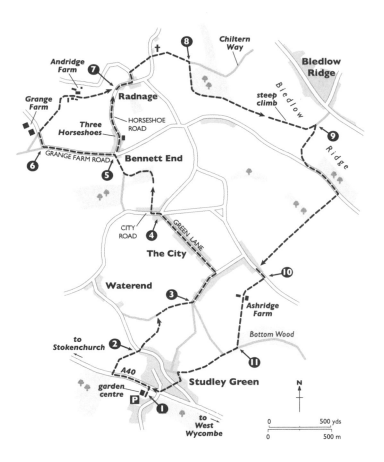

the path through the wood, indicated by the white arrows on the trees, until you reach the lane.

2. Cross the road bearing slightly right and take the drive before the house. When the drive bears right to garages continue ahead on a narrow footpath heading uphill. Continue as the path runs mainly between fences and hedges for about 300m (330yd) until a gravel track is reached giving access to a house on the right. Cross the track and follow the fenced footpath to the right between trees until the path reaches a junction of footpaths and bridleways at the end of a tarmac road.

3. Bear left on to the road and follow it for nearly 300m (330yd) until your reach Green Lane on the left. Walk the full length of Green Lane for 700m (766yd) to a T-junction.

4. Turn left here on to the oddly named City Road and after 80m (87yd) turn right on to a footpath by a war memorial. Follow this path for 500m (550yd) initially gently downhill and later more steeply downhill as the path bears left through a wood. Near the end of the wood at a junction with a bridleway from the left continue ahead more gently downhill. After a further 100m (110yd) bear right on to a gravel track giving access to a house on the left, eventually reaching the road at Bennett End.

5. From here you can either take a shortcut, stopping off at The Three Horseshoes pub along the way, or continue with your walk. For refreshments, continue straight ahead up Horseshoe Road for 100m (110yd) to the pub on the right. Upon leaving the pub, turn right and carry on along the road for 400m (440yd) until you rejoin the walk at point 7 on the map, where a footpath marked Chiltern Way joins on the left just as the road starts to go downhill (go straight to direction 7, below). Alternatively, to continue the main walk from Bennett End, turn left and follow Grange Farm Road for about 550m (600yd).

6. Turn right where the road splits and head towards Grange Farm. Just before the farm turn right on to a footpath signposted Chiltern Way. Follow the

RED KITES

Red kites are magnificent birds of prey with a distinctive forked tail, reddish plumage and a wingspan of nearly 2m (6½ft). Human persecution had driven these once common birds to extinction in England by the end of the 19th century. People thought they were a threat to game rearing and sheep farming, but in fact they usually scavenge on carrion, or feed on insects, earthworms or small mammals. A reintroduction project in the early 1990s led by the RSPB and English Nature saw over 90 birds re-introduced to the Chilterns from Spain, and now over 250 pairs are breeding here. The area around Studley Green is a particularly good place to look out for red kites because it lies close to where the birds were first reintroduced.

path up the hill, past the telegraph pole and through the gap in the hedge at the top. Continue to follow the Chiltern Way – signed after 20m (22yd) to the right – over stiles and crossing a small tarmac lane. Veer right down a tarmac drive, past Andridge Farm buildings and cottages and a line of conifers. Bear left and carry on until you reach the road, then turn left and carry on.

7. Follow the road to the junction and turn left. After 50m (55yd) turn right along the drive of Kirk Stile house, and follow the footpath, right, towards the church, across the road and into the churchyard. Cross the churchyard towards the back and over a stone stile in the wall and follow the Chiltern Way across two fields.

8. Where the path splits, bear right (leaving the Chiltern Way) and aim for the right-hand side of the wood. Follow the path between the field and the wood, then after the wood continue to follow the path along the slope for

0.8km (½ mile) ignoring other paths. Eventually you will come to a waymark where the path leaves the field edge and climbs up another steep hill towards Bledlow Ridge.

9. When you reach the junction with a bridleway turn right on to the bridleway back down into the valley until you reach the road at the bottom. Turn left along the road and then turn right after 350m (383yd) on to the footpath (ignoring the bridleway before this). At the end of the footpath you reach a road. Turn left and follow the road for 50m (55yd).

10. Turn right on to a footpath through a gate, just before Ashridge Farm drive. Cross the field and head for the right-hand end of the large barn. Pass through the gate, marked with an arrow, and straight on past the pond and down the track, through the farmyard. Carry on across the next field between the hedge and the fence and pass through the kissing gate, then go over a stile into a sunken path into Bottom Wood Nature Reserve, home to the common dormouse. Carry on downhill though Bottom Wood until you meet the main bridleway leading back towards Studley Green.

11. Turn right and follow the bridleway. Leave the wood, bearing left through a gate along a wide path between two fields and through another gate at the end. Turn sharp left uphill at the side of a house called Two Ways. After 50m (55yd), opposite a cottage called The Cottage, there is a gap in the hedge on the right. Go through it and follow the path across a tarmac road and between the gardens of two houses. You will come out on to the A40 through the gate of a house called Nutfield. Turn right and follow the footpath of the A40 until you reach the garden centre. Cross the road with care.

Courtesy of The Chilterns Area of Outstanding Natural Beauty.
For similar walks go to www.chilternsaonb.org

Henley Boots and Boats

HENLEY, HAMBLEDEN AND ASTON

*This flexible route enables you to explore the beautiful
Henley area – home to the Royal Regatta – either combining
a scenic boat trip with a short walk of 3.5km (2¼ miles), or
walking a neat 8km (5 miles) circuit. There's also the option of an
extension to the picturesque village of Hambleden. The afternoon
boat trip (Easter–30th September only) will take you upriver from
Henley to Marsh Lock, then back downstream to Hambleden Lock
near Mill End. When you buy your ticket, explain that you
are a walker and want to be dropped off at Mill End to
receive a walkers' discount.*

DISTANCE:	3.5–12km (2¼–7½ miles) (linear/circular)
TIME:	Allow 2–4½ hours (depending on route taken)
LEVEL:	Easy (along Thames Path) to moderate
START/PARKING:	Hart Street, Henley-on-Thames (RG9 2AR). OS grid reference SU758825 (OS Explorer map 171). Parking widely available in Henley. Boat trips leave from Station Road and are one-way only: contact Hobbs of Henley Ltd, 01491 572035 or see www.hobbsofhenley.com
GETTING THERE:	*By car:* Leave M4 at junction 9 on to A404(M) towards Henley, turning left on to A4130 *By public transport:* By train to Henley-on-Thames
REFRESHMENTS:	Pubs and cafés in Henley, The Stag & Huntsman, Hambleden, or The Flower Pot in Aston
LOCAL ATTRACTIONS:	Henley River and Rowing Museum; Greys Court
NOTES:	It is not possible to do this walk during the Henley Regatta and Festival. If you take the boat, tell the captain you want to be dropped off at Mill End as the boat does not stop automatically

DIRECTIONS

1. From Hart Street cross the bridge over the River Thames. Once over the bridge turn left, following the signs for the Thames Path to Hambleden Lock – the path between the buildings will take you on to the side of the river. Follow the path, keeping the river on your left. Along the way you will pass Fawley Court on the opposite bank. The house was designed by Sir Christopher Wren in 1684 to replace an earlier house that was badly damaged by Royalist troops during the Civil War. Wildlife to look out for includes red kites, buzzards, herons, kingfishers, pheasants and deer.

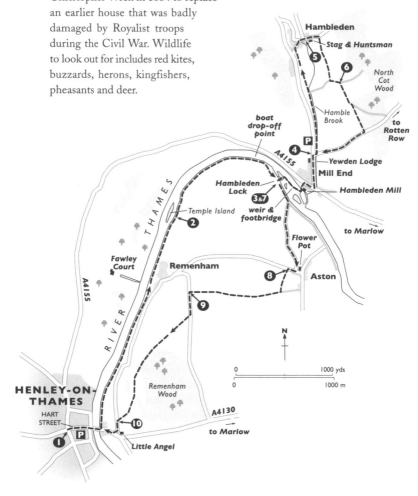

2. A little further on lies Temple Island with its delightful temple, designed by James Wyatt in 1771 as a summerhouse and fishing lodge for Fawley Court. The temple marks the start of the Regatta course. After following the path for 3.5km (2¼ miles) you will reach Hambleden Lock. If you choose to take the boat instead of walking, you will be dropped off just before the lock, as marked on the map. The beautiful building on the far side of the river is Hambleden Mill, mentioned in the Doomsday Book (1086) and only closed in 1995. Today the mill contains private apartments.

3. At Hambleden Lock you can either retrace your steps back to Henley, or return via Aston village (go straight to direction 7 below). Alternatively, for the extension to Hambleden, cross over the River Thames on a series of bridges and then follow the driveway to the main road. Take care crossing the road, then turn right and then left to follow the road towards Hambleden.

4. At the junction with the road off to the right leading to Rotten Row, enter the field through the kissing gate (note: there are toilets in the car park 50m (55yd) further along the Hambleden road if required). Follow the path through the valley towards the village, crossing a track halfway. Join the road, turning right over the stream and walk into the village.

5. Continue past The Stag and Huntsman pub and the private road sign, and carry on up the hill. Turn right on to the unsurfaced farm track before the buildings and follow the track back along the valley towards the River Thames. After 0.4km (¼ mile) the track forms a T-junction with another track. Turn left here, following the public footpath signs uphill.

6. Follow the footpath where it turns right along the hedge. Enter the wood through a kissing gate and bear right where the footpath forks, continuing through the kissing gate and across the field, then parallel to the wood. Follow this path until you reach the road at a stile. Turn right and follow the road down the hill to the junction at point 4. Turn left and walk back to Hambleden Lock. Retrace your steps over the bridges to the far bank at points 3/7.

7. From here you can either turn right and follow the Thames Path back to Henley or turn left and return via Aston. (If you didn't make the trip to Hambleden, just continue straight ahead.) For Aston, follow the Thames Path downriver towards Hurley along the road. Continue to follow the road as it bears right away from the river to the village of Aston. Bear left at the fork and, at the main road, turn left to go to The Flower Pot pub. Otherwise, turn right and follow the road for 50m (55yd).

8. Turn left at the permitted footpath sign and follow the track up the slope (the Copas Partnership has kindly given permission to use this section of path which is not a public right of way). Then turn right and follow the public footpath for 0.8km (½ mile).

9. At the road turn left and walk for about 200m (220yd), then turn right and follow the footpath across the field. Continue to follow the footpath through Remenham Wood. Leave the wood over the stile and cross the field to the signpost. Follow the path through the trees, and continue over the stiles and fields until you reach the outskirts of Henley.

10. At the road, turn left and follow the road past the cricket pitch until you reach the main road and The Little Angel pub. Turn right along the main road and cross the River Thames back into Henley.

Courtesy of The Chilterns Area of Outstanding Natural Beauty.
For similar walks go to www.chilternsaonb.org

A ROYAL EVENT

The famous Henley Royal Regatta is an annual five-day rowing event staged over the first weekend in July. The first regatta at Henley dates back to 1839, when an afternoon's boat racing was staged as part of a bigger public attraction that included a fair and other amusements. The regatta proved so popular that the following year it took place over two full days, increasing to three days in 1886, four in 1906 and five in 1986. Prince Albert became the regatta's first royal patron in 1851, after which the event became known as the Henley Royal Regatta. Since Albert's death, all subsequent monarchs have agreed to act as patron.

Whitchurch Hill Walk

WHITCHURCH HILL, PATH HILL AND COLLINS END

*This walk starts in the rural village of Whitchurch Hill,
which sits on the edge of the Chilterns Area of Outstanding
Natural Beauty, some 100m (330ft) above sea level. A moderate
walk over mixed farmland and woodland, it passes through some
lovely Chilterns scenery and affords wonderful views of the
surrounding landscape, including the Thames Valley. There are
a couple of short steep sections between Path Hill and Collins End,
but on the whole the route is easy going with no stiles to negotiate,
and your return is rewarded by welcome refreshments at a
traditional country pub.*

DISTANCE:	6.5km (4 miles) (extended figure 8)
TIME:	Allow 2–2½ hours
LEVEL:	Moderate (with a couple of short, steep climbs but no stiles)
START/PARKING:	The Sun Inn at Whitchurch Hill (RG8 7PU). Park in pub car park, preferably in the field at the back (do not park on grass verges in front and adjacent to pub). OS grid reference SU643793 (OS Explorer map 159). Alternative parking available at recreation ground
GETTING THERE:	*By car:* From Reading, take A329 to Pangbourne, then turn right on to B471 to Whitchurch Hill *By public transport:* Train to Reading, then take bus no. 142 (not Sundays), alighting at Hill Bottom, opposite Sun Inn
REFRESHMENTS:	The Sun Inn, Whitchurch Hill
LOCAL ATTRACTIONS:	Mapledurham House and Watermill

DIRECTIONS

1. With your back to the pub, turn right up the road and after a few metres turn left down an alleyway and into Oakdown Close. At the end of the close turn right and walk past Butler's Farm to Whitchurch Hill recreation ground.

2. After reaching the recreation ground take a footpath to the left and walk past some cottages to a kissing gate. Go through the gate and cross the meadow to another kissing gate. Go through, turn right and continue straight on, ignoring a footpath to the left. There are good views of the Thames Valley on this stretch of the path.

3. Continue straight ahead until you reach a byway. Turn left here and then after a few metres turn right through a wooden kissing gate. Walk straight ahead across the field, taking time to appreciate the views to your right. Pass through another wooden kissing gate and walk past the cottages.

4. At Path Hill continue along the road past more cottages until you reach a junction, where you turn right. Follow the road as it bends round to the left, ignoring the first path to the left. Carry on for about 200m (220yd) and opposite Path Hill Farm take a footpath to the left via a five-barred gate.

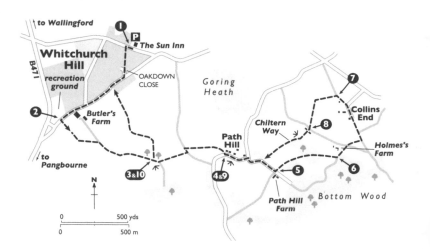

50

5. Cross the paddock to a metal gate. Once through the gate, walk straight down into the valley and, near the bottom, pass through a metal kissing gate on the right. Bearing slightly to your right, go up the hill to another kissing gate and follow the path through the wood. Pass through another gate and walk up to Holmes's Farm. After passing through another gate, bear right and follow the path round the perimeter of a wooden building to arrive at a track.

6. Turn left and, after a short distance, turn right on to a wide track. Walk along the track to a T-junction, turn left and walk straight ahead into the hamlet of Collins End. Where the road bears right, follow the bridleway straight ahead.

7. Continue along the bridleway for a short distance and then take the footpath to the left, passing through a wooden gate and on to a footpath that runs between a hedge and barbed wire. At the end of the hedge bear half left and follow the path diagonally across the field to a pair of cottages.

8. Go straight ahead, following the Chiltern Way sign, through a five-barred gate and across a meadow for a short while until you come to a metal kissing gate. Pass through this and follow the path downhill to a wooden kissing gate. Carry on down into the valley, then climb up the hill to another wooden kissing gate. Walk through a small copse to rejoin the road you were on earlier. Turn right and then left at the T-junction, retracing your steps back past the cottages at Path Hill.

9. Take the path on the right, leading past the end of the cottages, and go through a wooden kissing gate. Cross the meadow to another kissing gate and turn left on to a byway. After a few metres take a footpath to the right and continue straight ahead, following the perimeter of the field until you reach a path off to the right.

10. Take this path, following it along the field edge, then through a gap in the hedge to the left. Continue to follow the path until you reach the road at Whitchurch Hill where you retrace your steps back to your starting point, turning right towards The Sun Inn, left into Oakdown Close, then through the alleyway and right at the top.

Courtesy of The Chilterns Area of Outstanding Natural Beauty.
For similar walks go to www.chilternsaonb.org

Goring Gap Walk

GORING AND HARTSLOCK NATURE RESERVE

*This lovely walk takes you through the Goring Gap and
on to the Chiltern Hills – an Area of Outstanding Natural Beauty.
Starting from the picturesque village of Goring, with its historic
flint buildings and wonderful riverside setting, you follow the
River Thames for about 2.5km (1½ miles), passing through a hay
meadow before making the short but steep climb into the Hartslock
Nature Reserve, from where you are rewarded with spectacular
views back towards Goring and the North Wessex Downs on the
far side of the river. You can now choose either to extend your walk
uphill across scenic farmland or head back to your starting point.*

DISTANCE:	6.5km (4 miles) (circular) or 9km (5½ miles) with extension
TIME:	Allow 2–2½ hours (2½–3½ with extension)
LEVEL:	Moderate, with steep uphill slope (option of shorter, easy route)
START/PARKING:	Goring and Streatley Station, Gatehampton Road, Goring (RG8 0EP), parking in station car park. (Alternative parking off Station Road, starting walk in High Street). OS grid reference SU602805 (OS Explorer map 171)
GETTING THERE:	*By car:* Off A329, 13km (8 miles) north-west of Reading. *By public transport:* By train to Goring and Streatley Station, exiting on to Gatehampton Road, or regular buses from Reading and Wallingford
REFRESHMENTS:	The Miller of Mansfield or cafés in Goring
LOCAL ATTRACTIONS:	Beale Wildlife Park and Gardens; Basildon Park (National Trust)

DIRECTIONS

1. With the station behind you, turn left along Gatehampton Road, passing a pub on your right, then turn left to cross the bridge over the railway. Walk down the High Street to the end of the village where the bridge crosses the Thames. Just before the bridge, on the left-hand side of the road, you will see a sign for the Thames Path; follow the sign alongside the bridge to the towpath. On your left is Goring Water Mill, depicted by William Turner in an unfinished painting that is now on display in Tate Britain in London. A mill has stood on this site since before 1086, when a corn mill was recorded. In 1895 the mill was converted to generate electricity. The present building is actually a replica of the older one it replaced in the 1920s.

2. Turn left along the towpath and follow the river on your right as it makes a large sweeping curve, keeping an eye out for kingfishers and red kites along the way. The path takes you through Little Meadow which is managed by the Goring and Streatley Environment Group, partly as a traditional hay

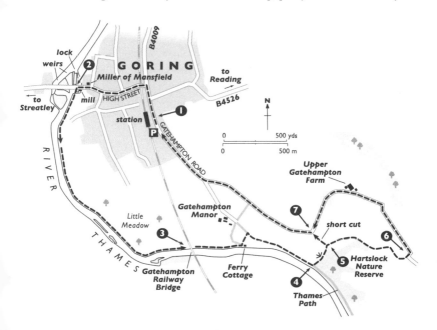

meadow and partly as a coppice for wildlife. After about 1.5km (1 mile) you reach an elegant brick railway bridge, designed during the 1830s by Isambard Kingdom Brunel as part of the Great Western Railway line between London and Bristol.

3. Walk under the bridge and continue along the towpath for about another 0.8km (½ mile), at which point the Thames Path turns left away from the river by the side of Ferry Cottage. Follow the path round and over the footbridge, turning right by the side of the horse paddocks. From here you get splendid views of the steep hills beyond, where the meltwaters burst through the chalk limestone half a million years ago to create the Goring Gap (see special feature, opposite). Continue along the path until you reach the edge of a wood. For those not wishing to make the short but steep uphill climb, you can retrace your steps back to Goring. Otherwise continue as below.

4. Turn sharp left at the edge of the wood and climb up to the gate on your left. Go through the gate into Hartslock Nature Reserve, named after a local family (the Harts) who owned a lock on the river beneath this point during the 1500s. The reserve is of national importance for its chalk grassland, and is home to a wide variety of plants, animals and fungi. Species specific to chalk grasslands include chalk milkwort, monkey and lady orchids, and the rare pasque flower (reintroduced to the site), plus many butterflies including the Adonis blue, a day-time moth (called a pyralid moth) and rare solitary bees. Once through the gate turn right along a steep footpath to the top of the hill from where you will be rewarded with splendid views over the river and hills beyond. Now walk downhill to the gate at the bottom of the field.

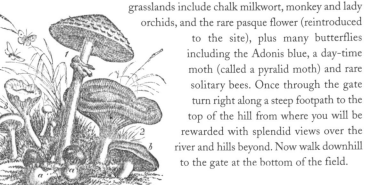

5. Go through the gate and on to the track beyond. Here you can either head back towards Goring, or continue your walk along the uphill scenic route. To head back, turn left along the track, following it for about 100m (110yd) until you reach a lane, at point 7 on the map (go to direction 7 below). For the scenic route, turn right and follow the track uphill for about 0.8km (½ mile).

6. At the footpath sign, opposite a gate, bear left on to a lane. Follow the lane as it bends sharply to the left and continue downhill past some farm buildings, looking out for hovering red kites along the way. Carry on through Upper Gatehampton Farm, passing to the left of the metal gate and bearing left to follow the lane steeply downhill.

7. At the bottom, follow the lane as it bends to the right (or, if you chose the shorter route, bear left on to the lane at this point). Carry along the road, ignoring the turn-off to Gatehampton Manor, and shortly after you enter the outskirts of Goring. Continue straight on along Gatehampton Road to return to the station and your starting point.

Courtesy of The Chilterns Area of Outstanding Natural Beauty.
For similar walks go to www.chilternsaonb.org

FORMING THE GORING GAP

Half a million years ago, the North Wessex Downs and the Chilterns formed a continuous chalk ridge, and the Thames, instead of flowing through Oxfordshire and on to London as it now does, veered north-east and flowed through East Anglia and into the North Sea near Ipswich. But with the coming of the Ice Age, a vast ice sheet pushed down from Scandinavia, turning the whole area into a frozen waste. When the ice finally melted, the meltwaters caused the river to become torrential and, with its old route still blocked by ice, the Thames changed its course and carved a new valley through the chalk ridge, forming what we know today as the Goring Gap.

Happy Valley Walk

OXFORD, SUNNINGWELL AND KENNINGTON

Setting out from south Oxford, this walk takes you along the lovely Chilswell Valley, one of the steepest valleys in the Oxford area and known locally as the Happy Valley. From here you climb Boars Hill, where Victorian poet and cultural critic Matthew Arnold loved to roam, and make a short detour to Jarn Mound to admire the fantastic views over Oxford. The route then takes you through the picturesque village of Sunningwell, where you may choose to stop for refreshments, then on through fields and meadows to Kennington. A brief amble along the Thames Path finally leads you back to your starting point.

DISTANCE:	14.5km (9 miles) (circular)
TIME:	Allow 4½ –5½ hours
LEVEL:	Moderate with some steep climbs
START/PARKING:	Redbridge park-and-ride car park on south end of Abingdon Road (A4144), Oxford (OX1 4XG). OS grid reference SP519036 (OS Explorer map 180, with short section on 170)
GETTING THERE:	*By car:* Take M40 turn-off to Oxford and merge on to A40; turn left at roundabout on to A4142 Eastern Bypass, and on to A423 Southern Bypass, turning right on to A4144 towards Oxford, then left on to Abingdon Road, with car park on left
	By public transport: By train to Oxford then number 35 or park-and-ride bus to Redbridge
REFRESHMENTS:	Fox Inn at Boars Hill or The Flowing Well at Sunningwell
LOCAL ATTRACTIONS:	Pitt Rivers Museum, Oxford; Didcot Railway Centre

DIRECTIONS

1. Leave the park-and-ride car park by the exit and turn left down Abingdon Road, following the footway over Hinksey Stream and the railway bridges. Turn right at the metal kissing gate on the right-hand side of the road and follow the footpath across the meadows to South Hinksey village.

2. At the lane turn right and follow it around to the left until you reach St Lawrence Road. Carry straight on, bearing left down Manor Road and

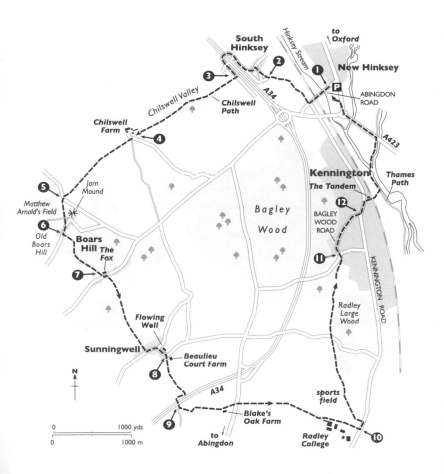

turning right at the T-junction at the end of the village. At the roundabout, bear right and, taking great care, follow the road round over the bridge and back down to where the road rejoins the dual carriageway. Carry straight ahead here, down the lane running parallel to the main road.

3. Take the next path on your right – the Chilswell Path – and follow it up the steep-sided Chilswell Valley, formed upstream by springs on Boars Hill that plunge into miniature gorges, created by erosion as the limestone is dissolved by rainwater. The valley is a local nature reserve, bought by the Oxford Preservation Trust in 2007, and contains a range of important habitats including a reed bed, mature woodland and limestone grassland. Look out for rock rose, sainfoin, bee orchid and pyramidal orchid along the way. Continue along the valley through the copse to Chilswell Farm.

4. From Chilswell Farm cross the metalled road, then go through the pedestrian gate and take the right fork bridleway across the field to a track. Follow the track as it turns into a narrow lane, passing between some houses and up to Boars Hill.

5. At the metalled road turn left and shortly afterwards turn right down a lane that leads around between Jarn Heath and Matthew Arnold's Field, which was purchased by the Oxford Preservation Trust in 1928. It was here that Matthew Arnold's celebrated Scholar Gypsy (from the poem of 1853) looked down on Oxford from the Cumnor-Hinksey ridge and 'Turn'd once to watch, while thick the snowflakes fall, the line of festal light in Christ Church hall'. Emerging on to a metalled lane, carry on straight ahead. (Alternatively, you can turn left and left again to take a short detour to Jarn Mound, from where you can admire the views across Matthew Arnold's Field and Oxford) At the next road junction bear right down the hill.

6. Turn left opposite Orchard Lane and turn right at the fork along the drive, leaving it by a signed narrow track through the trees. On emerging from the trees continue along the field edge to the road.

7. Turn left uphill and, just past 'Pinewood' and opposite The Fox public house, take the narrow lane to the right. At the path junction keep right and carry straight on to a long residential drive, at the end of which is a footpath that

crosses the field into Sunningwell. Turn left on to the road into the village, past the duck pond and round to the right as the road goes uphill past The Flowing Well public house.

8. At the bend in the road, just before Beaulieu Court Farm, take the bridleway on the right, leading down a farm lane and past some converted barns. Continue along the bridleway and just after crossing the bridge over the A34 take the footpath that leads down some steps.

9. Follow the footpath as it turns left up a lane and through Blake's Oak Farm, and carry straight on until you reach the old Abingdon road. Cross over with care and continue straight ahead through the avenue of chestnut trees to Radley College. The route then runs along the college drive down to the college entrance gates at the Kennington Road.

10. Turn left at the entrance gates, then left again just after the bus stop, back into the college grounds. Follow the path as it bears right, across the sports field and then along beside a small copse on your right. Continue along the path across the fields to a lane opposite Radley Large Wood. Cross the lane and carry straight ahead, keeping the wood on your right to begin with, then on your left as you walk up the hill, finally reaching the road.

11. Cross and take the road opposite (Bagley Wood Road) and continue along the lane as it narrows to a path and then rejoins the Bagley Wood Road. Follow the road down the hill to its junction with Kennington Road.

12. Turn left along Kennington Road for a short distance, then turn right down the lane that runs alongside The Tandem public house. Cross the bridge over the railway, and continue across the meadow to the Thames Path. Turn left and follow the towpath under the Eastern Bypass and then turn left up the bank to a cycle track. Turn right and follow the cycle track to the underpass. In the middle of the roundabout turn right and follow the route back to the park-and-ride car park.

Courtesy of Oxfordshire County Council. For similar walks see www.oxfordshire.gov.uk/walksandrides

The Hamptons Loop

KIDLINGTON, THRUPP AND
SHIPTON-ON-CHERWELL

*This charming walk along the Cherwell Valley, just north of
Oxford, takes you across fields and meadows to Hampton Poyle and
Hampton Gay, linking up at its furthest point with the Oxford
Canal at Shipton-on-Cherwell. From here you follow the canal
back to the tiny hamlet of Thrupp, where waterside refreshments
await you. The canal makes a right-angled turn at this point,
continuing on its way to join up with the Thames at Oxford,
while your path takes you back through woodland and
open fields alongside the pretty River Cherwell to
your starting point in Kidlington.*

DISTANCE:	5.5km (3½ miles) (circular)
TIME:	Allow 1½– 2 hours
LEVEL:	Easy
START/PARKING:	Car park behind St Mary's Church in Church Street, Kidlington (OX5 2BB). OS grid reference SP497148 (OS Explorer map 180)
GETTING THERE:	*By car:* Turn off M40 at junction 8 and merge on to A40; follow A40 over first roundabout, then take third exit at Cutteslowe Roundabout on to A4165; go straight ahead at next roundabout on to A4260 into Kidlington, and turn right on to Green Road, then left into School Road; bear right into High Street and continue up Church Street to the church
	By public transport: By train to Oxford, then catch bus no. 7A or 7B to Kidlington
REFRESHMENTS:	Annie's Tea Room or The Boat Inn, Thrupp
LOCAL ATTRACTIONS:	Blenheim Palace

DIRECTIONS

1. St Mary's Church provides a picturesque starting point for this walk. The present church dates from c.1220 with later alterations, and sits on the foundations of an earlier church of Norman or Saxon origin. Known as Our Lady's Needle, its slender spire rises over 52m (171km) and is a local landmark. Opposite the church stand Lady Ann Morton's Almshouses, built by Sir William Morton in 1671 in memory of his wife. If you investigate, look out for the Morton arms on the north gable end and the names of some of Morton's children over the windows. From the entrance barrier to the car park, walk through the wooden kissing gate and follow the stoned footpath straight ahead, through the woodland nature reserve and over the footbridge by the pond.

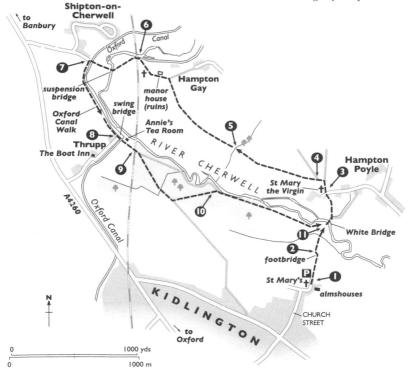

FROM HEAVY GOODS TO HOLIDAYS

Completed in 1790, the 124km (77 mile) long Oxford Canal linked Oxford with Coventry, so providing a continuous waterway between Birmingham and London by way of the Midlands canal system and the River Thames. During the 19th century this was an important route for the transportation of coal, lime and stone. The coal trade was the last vestige of this formerly diverse traffic, declining in the 1950s with the last regular deliveries made in 1961. Soon, however, a new industry was taking over from the old coal trade – tourism – and in 1971 the wharf at Thrupp was lengthened to accommodate the increasing number of pleasure boats passing up and down the canal.

2. Turn right after the footbridge and keep to the right-hand edge of the fields, following the path to the River Cherwell. Cross White Bridge and bear left, taking the path across the fields, through gates and over stiles, until you reach the road by St Mary the Virgin Church at Hampton Poyle.

3. Cross the road by the church and continue straight ahead into the field. Cross into the next field over a stile and then bear left, crossing over two more stiles 20m (22yd) up on the left-hand side.

4. Walk diagonally right across the next paddock to the far corner. Carry on across the next field heading in the same direction to a stile and footbridge in the top left-hand corner. Cross over and walk straight across the next field towards the small spinney where you cross another footbridge.

5. Cross the next field and go over the stile, then follow the path across another field. Cross the stile on the far side by a large ash tree and head towards the ruins of a manor house (to the right of the church). Built by the Barry family in the 16th century, this house retained its original Elizabethan plan and features almost unaltered until it was destroyed by fire in 1887, since when it has remained a ruin. Bear left, heading towards a kissing gate just before Hampton Gay church, and follow the path to the riverside.

6. Continue under the railway bridge and bear left, crossing the field diagonally. Cross the suspension bridge over the River Cherwell and walk through the next field, crossing the stile beside the metal gate. Follow the lane to the canal bridge and cross over into Shipton-on-Cherwell. In 1874, a nearby railway crash was the worst accident in the history of the Great Western Railway, with more than 30 people killed and 70 injured. At the time there was a rumour that a curse had been put on the local manor house because the family in residence had refused to help rescue victims from the wreckage.

7. Once over the bridge, turn left along the towpath and follow the Oxford Canal Walk southwards towards Thrupp. After a left-hand bend, the canal widens considerably into what is known as the Thrupp Wide. Upon reaching Thrupp, however, it makes a sharp right-hand turn and becomes very narrow.

8. At Thrupp, cross over the swing bridge and follow the path through the British Waterways yard past the cottages and on towards the railway line. Better still, now might be a good time to stop for a little light refreshment.

9. Pass under the railway line and through the gate, then head straight on for 30m (33yd) before bearing diagonally right through the woods. (Alternatively, you could just carry straight on along on the mown path, with the River Cherwell on your left, until you reach point 10 on the map.) Follow the woodland path for about 200m (220yd) until you see a small bridge and a waymarked post. Go straight on, then bear left back towards the river. When you reach the main path by the river turn right.

10. Follow the path straight on through the woods, then alongside the river through a field. This is a good place to watch out for kingfishers. Other wildlife to look out for along the walk includes muntjac deer, rabbits and foxes, to mention but a few. After about 1km (²/₃ mile) you will reach White Bridge, which you crossed on your way out.

11. At White Bridge, you should retrace your steps back to your starting point at St Mary's Church in Kidlington.

Courtesy of Buckinghamshire County Council. For more information go to www.buckscc.gov.uk/bcc/row/walks.page

The Trout Inn Walk

EYNSHAM, SWINFORD AND WOLVERCOTE

This delightful Oxfordshire-based walk starts in the market town of Eynsham, mentioned in the Anglo-Saxon Chronicle as 'Egonesham'. The route takes you down to the historic Swinford Toll Bridge, then follows the Thames Path as it heads east towards Oxford. Your destination is the The Trout – a famous riverside inn at Wolvercote beloved by Lewis Caroll and CS Lewis, and featured in the Inspector Morse novels. From here you return across fields and alongside the beautiful Wytham Wood to your starting point. The path is waymarked on gates and stiles, and at every change of direction, making it easy to follow.

DISTANCE:	13km (8 miles) (partly circular)
TIME:	Allow 4–5 hours
LEVEL:	Moderate (with several stiles and steep slopes)
START/PARKING:	Eynsham car park, reached via Clover Place or Back Lane (OX29 4QP). OS grid reference SP430093 (OS Explorer map 180)

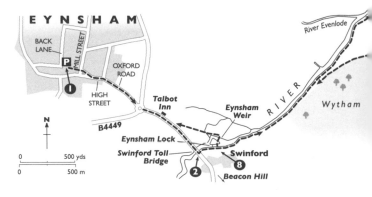

GETTING THERE: *By car:* Heading west, turn off A40 from Oxford.
  By public transport: By train to Oxford, then
  catch bus no. 51 towards Witney, or no. 18
  towards Bampton
REFRESHMENTS: The Trout Inn, Wolvercote
LOCAL ATTRACTIONS: Cogges Manor Farm Museum; North Leigh
  Roman Villa

DIRECTIONS

1. The walk starts in the centre of Eynsham, once the site of an 11th-century Benedictine Abbey that was one of the most important abbeys in England. The monastery was disbanded by Henry VIII in 1538 and, when its remains were finally pulled down in the 17th century, many of the old stones were used to construct new houses in the village, some of which remain to this day. Leave by the back of the car park, by the Eynsham parish council noticeboard, following the sign for the village centre down the walled lane into Mill Street. Continue directly across Mill Street into Thames Street, bearing left into the

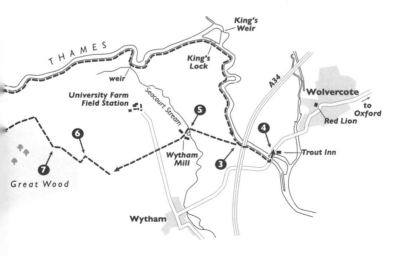

High Street and on to the Oxford Road. Carry straight down this road, out of the village, across the roundabout (crossing with care), and past The Talbot Inn until you reach Swinford Toll Bridge, one of the most beautiful bridges on the Thames.

2. Cross the bridge and immediately turn left down on to the towpath. To your right, beyond Swinford, lies Beacon Hill, a 122m (135yd) knoll that was allegedly fortified by Offa of Mercia in AD 779 to defend the 'Swine Ford'. During the 16th century, the summit housed one of the beacons set up to warn of the approach of the Spanish Armada. Today, the hill houses an underground reservoir with two 22.5 megalitre (5 million gallon) tanks, 9m (30ft) deep, which supply drinking water to the surrounding area. Follow the Thames Path away from the bridge for about 5.5km (3½ miles), passing alongside the lock at Eynsham Weir and over the weir bridge of Seacourt Stream. Further on you will pass the lock at King's Weir, after which the river changes general direction, heading south towards Oxford.

3. At the point where the A34 Oxford ring road bridges the Thames, you can either carry on to the famous Trout Inn at Wolvercote, or turn sharply to your right and continue your walk back across the fields towards Swinford (go straight to direction 4, below). To reach The Trout, carry on down the Thames Path a short way until you reach the old bridge over the river: the pub is on the far side.

4. From The Trout, retrace your steps to point 3 on the map and take the left-hand fork towards Wytham Mill. Cross the field to a stile and a footbridge, then carry straight on to the next bridge. Cross the bridge and bear left.

5. Follow the track between the Wytham Mill buildings and carry on to the metalled road (which leads to the University Farm Field Station). Go straight over the road and follow the path along the edge of the fields to the far corner. Bear right through the gap in the hedge and carry on across two more fields.

6. Turn left and then right to follow the track along the edge of Wytham Great Wood. A Site of Special Scientific Interest (SSSI) and one of the finest woods in England, Wytham was given to the University of Oxford in 1943, since when it has become home to the world's longest-running ecological study.

With areas of yew, beech and mixed ash and sycamore, the wood supports fallow, muntjac and roe deer, while populations of badgers and great tits form the focus of study for the University's Conservation Research Unit. Parts of the wood also provided inspiration to JRR Tolkien for aspects of the Old Forest in *The Lord of the Rings*.

7. After a while, the path leaves the edge of the wood, bearing right to take you along the edge of a field until you reach a stile. Cross the stile and turn left on to the field edge. Continue walking alongside the woods until you rejoin the Thames Path. Carry on to Eynsham Lock.

8. At Eynsham Lock you have a choice of routes: you can either continue retracing your steps to the car park, or you can follow the signed permissive route over the weir. If you take the latter route, bear left after crossing the weir and cross the small bridge over the stream. Then cut diagonally across the field to take you back to the Oxford Road. Turn right past The Talbot Inn and retrace your steps to the car park or bus stop.

Courtesy of Oxfordshire County Council. For similar walks see
www.oxfordshire.gov.uk/walksandrides

BRIDGE FOR SALE

The lovely Swinford Toll Bridge was built by the 4th Earl of Abingdon under a special Act of Parliament of 1767, which allowed for the replacement of an ancient ferry. The ferry crossing was often hazardous and, in 1636, the ferry carrying a group of Welsh sheriffs delivering ship money to Charles I capsized and several people drowned. Opened to traffic in 1769, the toll bridge turned out to be quite a money-spinner, especially since according to the act all income derived from it was exempt from tax. When it came up for sale in 2009, the bridge was bringing in £190,000 a year – tax-free! The down side was that it cost over £1 million for the privilege.

Walking The Ridgeway

THE DEVIL'S PUNCHBOWL, LETCOMBE BASSETT, LETCOMBE REGIS AND SEGSBURY CAMP

Set within the North Wessex Downs Area of Outstanding Natural Beauty, just south of the Thames Valley, this walk takes you along a wonderful stretch of The Ridgeway National Trail through some classic undulating downland scenery. Starting out near the Devil's Punchbowl – a large natural amphitheatre – the path leads down to the picturesque villages of Letcombe Bassett and Letcombe Regis before heading south for the steep climb back up the down. Here you have the opportunity to explore the Iron Age fort of Segsbury Camp, from where you get tremendous views to the north, before making your way back along the Ridgeway to your starting point.

DISTANCE:	12km (7½ miles) (circular) or shorter route of 8km (5 miles)
TIME:	3½–4½ hours (shorter route: 2½–3 hours)
LEVEL:	Moderate, with one steep climb
START/PARKING:	Car park on The Ridgeway at Sparsholt Firs, on south side of B4001, 6.5km (4 miles) north of Lambourn (Lambourn post code: RG17 8YG). OS grid reference SU343851 (OS Explorer map 170)
GETTING THERE:	*By car:* Exit M4 at junction 14 heading north on to A338 towards Wantage; follow B4000 left to Lambourn then bear right on to B4001 *By public transport:* See www.traveline.org.uk for details
REFRESHMENTS:	The Greyhound, Letcombe Regis
LOCAL ATTRACTIONS:	The Vale and Downland Museum, Wantage

DIRECTIONS

1. From the car parking area on The Ridgeway walk south-east, away from the telecommunications mast, along the Trail for just over 500m (550yd).

2. At the old wooden stile turn sharp left across the field and descend a little to a kissing gate above the Devil's Punchbowl. This natural feature is a dramatic dry valley or coombe, which has been sculpted in the past by the action of water. Nowadays it is a great grassy amphitheatre and, as one of the largest expanses of unimproved chalk grassland in the area, much of it is protected as a Site of Special Scientific Interest.

3. Go through the gate, turn right and keep to the upper slope, following the fence. At the end of the first field go through the kissing gate and continue in the same direction, still keeping to the upper slope next to the fence.

4. About 75m (82yd) after the fence ends, bear left down the grass field and go through the kissing gate. Head down the steep slope to the field gate on the opposite side of the field to the right of the trees.

5. Follow the fence around the bottom of the slope for approximately 1.5km (1 mile) through several fields, including a short dogleg right and then left at the end of the first field. When you reach a hedge, turn left down the track towards Letcombe Bassett. This village was established in Saxon times and many of the cottages are timber-framed and thatched. In Thomas Hardy's

Jude the Obscure, Letcombe Bassett is the village of Cresscombe, named after the old cress beds on the brook just down the road from point 10 on the map.

6. When the track joins the open field, turn right and go through the gate and along the lane passing St Michael and All Angels Church on your right, which dates from the 12th century and has a Norman doorway and chancel arch. At the junction, turn right and walk uphill.

7. Just before the lane bends to the right you have a choice of two routes: you can either take the short route back to The Ridgeway or carry on towards Letcombe Regis. For the shorter option, continue up the lane, forking right at the junction. At the top of the hill turn right along The Ridgeway to take you back to your starting point. For the longer route, turn left up the steep bank and head across the small field to the right edge of the brick wall ahead. Go over the stile and follow the tarmac drive down towards the road.

8. Just before the road, take the footpath that rises gently to the right and then follow an enclosed path with views of the Letcombe Brook and meadows.

9. When the path joins the bridleway, turn right through the gate and follow the bridleway towards the hills rising in the distance. Alternatively, you can turn left here to visit Letcombe Regis and The Greyhound pub, a short walk away.

10. At the end of the fenced path, go through the kissing gate and bear slightly left, climbing steeply up to the kissing gate in the top left corner of the field.

BRITAIN'S OLDEST ROAD

The Ridgeway is one of only 15 National Trails in England and Wales. It is thought to be the oldest road in the country, having been in existence since Neolithic (New Stone Age) times some 5,000 years ago, and is surrounded by numerous prehistoric sites. Starting in the Avebury World Heritage Site it travels for 139km (87 miles) in a north-easterly direction along a chalk ridge, bisected at roughly the mid-point by the River Thames and finishing in an Iron Age fort on top of Ivinghoe Beacon. Throughout its length it passes through fine countryside: to the west of the Thames it traverses the open, rolling and remote downland of the North Wessex Downs Area of Outstanding Natural Beauty, and to the east it crosses the more wooded and intimate landscape of the Chilterns.

11. Beyond the gate, bear left to Segsbury Camp and then right to follow the fence around it. Go through the kissing gate and right on to the track to reach The Ridgeway after 50m (55yd). Alternatively, if you want to explore Segsbury Camp, go over the stile on the opposite side of the track. Also known as Letcombe Castle, Segsbury Camp is one of several Iron Age forts that line the western half of The Ridgeway. Excavations in the 1990s established that the fort was densely occupied by roundhouses throughout the Iron Age, and that it was largely domestic in function. There are tremendous views north from the ramparts.

12. Turn right on to The Ridgeway and follow this for almost 4.5km (3 miles) back to the start. If you are there relatively early, you may well see racehorses training on the gallops to the south.

Courtesy of Natural England/The Ridgeway National Trail/North Wessex Down AONB. For more information and similar walks see www.nationaltrail.co.uk/ridgeway

White Horse Walk

WHITE HORSE HILL, UFFINGTON CASTLE
AND ASHDOWN ESTATE

*Situated to the south of the Thames Valley, beyond the Vale of
White Horse, this beautiful walk takes you across the North Wessex
Downs, along an ancient and enigmatic stretch of The Ridgeway –
Britain's oldest road. Leaving the 21st century behind for a few
hours, the route takes you to the famous White Horse of Uffington,
etched into the hillside 3,000 years ago, then on past an Iron Age
hill fort and a Neolithic long barrow. Further on you have a
chance to explore the Ashdown Estate, with its tales of lost love and
World War II inhabitants, before heading back along the chalk
ridges, with their magnificent views, to your starting point.*

DISTANCE:	**12km (7½ miles) (circular)**
TIME:	**Allow 3½–4½ hours**
LEVEL:	**Moderate (with one steep climb)**
START/PARKING:	**Car park at White Horse Hill, near Uffington (Uffington post code: SN7 7RP). OS grid reference SU293866 (OS Explorer map 170)**
GETTING THERE:	***By car:* Turn off the B4507 Wantage/Swindon road as signposted**
	***By public transport:* Train to Swindon, then Swindon/Lambourn bus no. 47 (not Sundays), alighting at Rose and Crown in Ashbury; walk 2.5km (1½ miles) south along B4000 to join walk just before point 5 on the map**
REFRESHMENTS:	**The Fox and Hounds, Uffington, or The Rose and Crown, Ashbury**
LOCAL ATTRACTIONS:	**Ashdown House (National Trust)**

DIRECTIONS

1. Leave the main car park by the gate nearest to the disabled bays and make your way across the field towards the White Horse. Head for the furthest gate on the left and, after crossing the road, follow the sign-posted path up to the White Horse. From the top of the hill, by the horse's head, look out

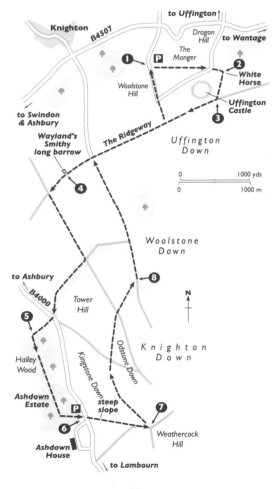

across the Vale of White Horse – on a clear day you can see over 22km (35 miles) away, to the Cotswold and Chiltern Hills.

2. Leave the White Horse by heading up the hill, passing Uffington Castle on your right – an Iron Age hill fort with a well-preserved rampart and ditch. In summer, many butterfly species can be seen along the route. Look out for the chalkhill blue, particularly around Uffington Castle and other sunny south-facing spots. Carry on until you reach The Ridgeway, an ancient route used since prehistoric times by travellers, cattle drovers and soldiers, and now a National Trail.

3. Turn right on to The Ridgeway and continue until you reach Wayland's Smithy on your right. This Neolithic long barrow (burial mound) is steeped in history and legend: it is said that a silver coin left among the stones will get your horse shod!

4. Continue on from Wayland's Smithy for 250m (275yd). At the crossroads, take the path to the left, passing a barn, and carry on until you reach the tree line. Turn right here and follow the footpath until you come to a road. Cross the road and follow the footpath straight ahead towards Hailey Wood. Walk alongside the edge of the wood until you reach a grassy avenue off to your left, which runs through Ashdown Estate.

5. Leave the footpath and walk along the large avenue towards Ashdown House. The house was built in the late 17th century by the 1st Earl of Craven who, it was said, was in love with Elizabeth, Queen of Bohemia. It was built to offer Elizabeth a refuge from plague-ridden London, but unfortunately she died of a disease in 1662 before ever setting eyes on her new home. The Earl of Craven lived into his late 80s and never married. Feel free to make detours and explore the woodland paths leading off the main avenue. These woods contain ancient beech pollards and dappled glades created by coppicing. Earth banks, thought to be Celtic field boundaries, run through the woods, and

you can also find outlines of buildings used by American soldiers during World War II when they occupied the house. When you near Ashdown House, head back on to the main avenue and follow the sign to the car park.

6. Continue onwards, crossing the road and climbing up Kingstone Down, keeping to the fence line. At the top of the hill head towards the weathercock from where you will get a rewarding view of the house. From here, with the house in front of you, go to the right and return to the path in the corner of the field, marked by a stile.

7. Follow this path across the field, keeping a view of Uffington Castle in the distance. Stay on the same path until you reach a small wood.

8. Turn left at the edge of the wood and follow the path until you reach The Ridgeway near Wayland's Smithy. Turn right and begin to retrace your steps back to the car park. If you prefer, instead of following the path back via Uffington Castle and the White Horse, take a short cut by turning left at the first road junction and following the lane back to the car park.

Courtesy of The National Trust. For similar walks go to www.nationaltrust.org.uk/walks

THE WHITE HORSE AT UFFINGTON

Dating from the Bronze Age, this stylized horse is thought to be the oldest chalk figure in Britain, although why it was created still remains a mystery. Although it looks like it has simply been etched into the chalk, it does in fact have a more complex construction, comprising deep trenches that have been infilled with chalk blocks. The White Horse is one of several chalk marks found in the southern chalk downs, others including the White Horse at Cherhill and the Cerne Abbas giant in Dorset. Left unattended, the marks soon green over. During the 18th and 19th centuries 'scouring fairs' were held on the hillside every seven years, during which local people would gather to clean the horse; since then, fresh chalk has been regularly compacted in to preserve the marks.

Barns and Bluebells

FARINGDON, GREAT COXWELL AND LITTLE COXWELL

*This scenic walk begins in the market town of
Faringdon (meaning fern-covered hill), which lies nestled on
the slopes of a hill overlooking the Thames Valley to the north-west
and the Vale of White Horse to the south-east. Heading west out of
the town, the waymarked path takes you across fields and through
woods awash with bluebells in the spring, then past the site of
an Iron Age fort and on to the beautiful 13th-century barn at
Great Coxwell, much beloved by William Morris. From
here you return to your starting point via the picturesque
villages of Great Coxwell and Little Coxwell.*

DISTANCE:	11km (7 miles) (circular)
TIME:	Allow 3$^{1}/_{2}$–4$^{1}/_{2}$ hours
LEVEL:	Moderate (with several stiles and slopes)
START/PARKING:	Market Place in Faringdon (SN7 7HL). OS grid reference SU289955 (OS Explorer map 170). Parking available off Gloucester Street and Southampton Street
GETTING THERE:	*By car:* Take A420 Oxford/Swindon road, turning north on to A417 into Faringdon *By public transport:* By train to Oxford or Swindon, then catch bus no. 66 to Faringdon
REFRESHMENTS:	The Old Crown Coaching Inn, Faringdon, or The Eagle Tavern, Little Coxwell
LOCAL ATTRACTIONS:	Farmer Gow's, Fernham, or Tom Brown's School Museum, Uffington

DIRECTIONS

1. Faringdon has been a market town since 1218 when King John granted it a royal charter to hold a weekly market. During the Civil War, it was one of the last places in England to hold out for the King, although Oliver Cromwell briefly occupied the town in 1645: the marks of cannon fire can still be seen on All Saints Church to the north of Market Place. Starting with your back to the Bell Hotel, turn left then take the right fork down Gloucester Street to the roundabout. Turn right here, then after a short distance cross over the road and turn left down Canada Lane. As the road bends, continue straight on to the rough surfaced lane.

2. Turn right on to the enclosed footpath leading to a gate. Go through the gate and follow the footpath as it cuts across the left corner of the field to another gate. Continue along the field edge and cross into the next field, bearing right where the path forks. Follow the electricity poles across the field to a bridge, and carry on along the edge of the field.

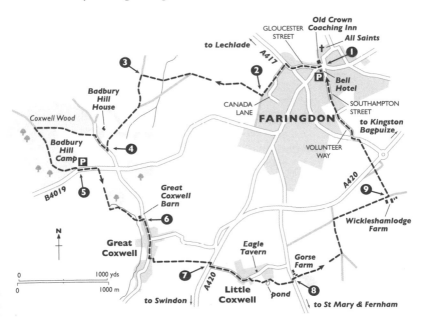

3. When you reach the bridleway, turn left and cross the field to a gate. Continue along the bridleway by the edge of the next field, then go straight uphill across a field, passing Badbury Hill House on your right.

4. When you reach the road, turn right and then left on to the footpath as it skirts round the edge of Coxwell Wood. Owned by the National Trust, this wood has one of the country's most spectacular displays of bluebells in springtime. When you reach the stile, cross over and continue straight on through the wood to another stile. After crossing, turn left uphill to Badbury Hill Camp – an Iron Age fort, strategically placed on the highest ground in the area. The banks of the camp were levelled early in the 19th century, leaving little but vestiges of the fosse (ditch) on the south side and a faint escarpment on the other sides. Follow the path around the camp and through the car park to the road.

5. Turn left down the road and after about 200m (220yd) turn right on to a footpath leading towards a copse of trees and Great Coxwell beyond. After 300m (330yd) bear left over a stile, keeping the copse on your left, and continue along the path as it bears right along the edge of a field to bring you to Great Coxwell Barn. This 13th-century Cistercian monastic barn was much admired by William Morris who called it 'unapproachable in its dignity' and frequently brought guests here to wonder at its structure. The barn was acquired by The National Trust in 1956 under the will of Ernest Cook and is open all year – it's well worth a look inside (see special feature, opposite).

6. Turn right along the road leading into Great Coxwell. Walk through the village and just past 'Hillside' take the clearly marked path to the left, dog-legging right and left and following the path across the field to the A420.

7. Cross the A420 with care, turning right and then left on to the old road leading into the picturesque village of Little Coxwell. (Here, a short detour will take you to the 12th-century church of St Mary, which boasts many

A Medieval Masterpiece

The Great Coxwell Barn is the only remaining part of a 13th-century grange that belonged to the monks of Beaulieu Abbey in Hampshire. Built of Cotswold stone with a slate roof, it has an exceptionally interesting timber construction that can be seen from the inside. Nearly all the timber beams, struts and posts are original, and the barn provides an awesome reminder of the skills and craftsmanship of medieval carpenters. Measuring 40 x 15m (131 x 49ft), it would have been the warehouse of the Middle Ages, used for storage of the various crops grown by the grange.

interesting architectural features.) To continue your walk, take the second signposted footpath on the right (signed Fernham) and follow the path through a garden and a kissing gate. Carry on along the field edge to another kissing gate, then go past a tennis court and a pond. Continue following the left-hand field edges until you reach a road.

8. Turn left and take the footpath on the right, by Gorse Farm. Follow the track through the gate and uphill to a stile, and then on until you reach a bridleway. Turn left and follow the bridleway downhill. Before reaching the A420, turn right on to another bridleway and carry on to Wickleshamlodge Farm.

9. Turn left on to the farm access track. As the track bends, carry straight on over a stile and carefully down towards the A420. Cross the road with care to the footpath on the opposite side, and carry straight on until you reach a road entering Faringdon. At the road, turn left then right down Volunteer Way. At Faringdon Business Centre follow the path straight on, ignoring the footpath sign to the left. Cross the road by Southampton Street car park and carry straight on to Market Place.

Courtesy of Oxfordshire County Council. For similar walks see www.oxfordshire.gov.uk/walksandrides

Willow Walk

BUSCOT AND KELMSCOTT

*This lovely walk takes you from the unspoilt village
of Buscot through fields and meadows to Kelmscott, where
Victorian designer and socialist William Morris once lived. Here
you can explore Morris's life and loves, visiting the church where
he lies buried, looking out for the famous stone plaque depicting
Morris beneath a tree, and viewing his much-loved summer
residence, Kelmscott Manor. Or you can simply stop off for some
light refreshment in a traditional country pub. Your return
route takes you along a stretch of the Thames that forms
part of the Willow Walk, once popular with Morris
and his artistic friends.*

DISTANCE:	6.5km (4 miles) (figure of 8) or shorter route of 4.5km (3 miles)
TIME:	Allow 2–2½ hours (shorter route: 1½–2 hours)
LEVEL:	Easy
START/PARKING:	Buscot Weir car park, in Buscot village (nearby post code: SN7 8DA). OS grid reference SU231977 (OS Explorer map 170)
GETTING THERE:	*By car:* Off A417 Wantage/Cirencester road, 3km (2 miles) south east of Lechlade *By public transport:* Train to Swindon, then take bus no. 64 (not Sundays) to Lechlade and follow the Thames Path to Buscot, joining the walk at point 9 on the map
REFRESHMENTS:	The Plough Inn, Kelmscott or Buscot village shop and tea room
LOCAL ATTRACTIONS:	Buscot Park House and Gardens (National Trust)

DIRECTIONS

1. From the car park, turn right and walk up the lane towards the lock. The second field on your left, where the ground looks uneven, is the site of old Buscot village, abandoned centuries ago probably as a result of the plague. Alongside the weir pool on your right, look out for a yellow waymark.

2. Follow the waymarked path sharp right back across the grassland surrounding the weir pool to the far corner. Cross a small footbridge and follow the edge of the field to a group of cottages on the site of Buscot Wharf. Note the shallow ditch that runs between the cottages and the river: this was once a 'cut' which allowed barges to deliver salt, coal and other 'dirty' cargoes to the Buscot Park Estate.

3. At the lane, turn right and walk down towards the junction with the main road. Just before the road, bear round to your left and follow the waymarks

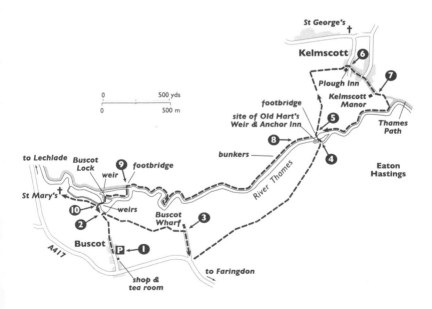

across the fields until you reach the site of The Anchor Inn and Old Hart's Weir at Eaton Hastings.

4. All that now remains at the site is a footbridge and a small outbuilding. The Anchor, which lay to the right of the bridge, was a very popular public house and campsite until it was destroyed by a tragic fire in 1980. The National Trust, which owns the land, decided to let the site go back to nature, and traces of the inn's foundations are all that remain. Old Hart's Weir was the last 'flash' lock (a lock with a single gate) and weir on the Thames. It was removed in 1936 to alleviate local flooding: traces of its concrete edge can still be seen upstream of the footbridge. Cross the river via the Eaton footbridge.

5. You now have a choice of routes: you can either turn left to follow the Thames Path back to Buscot (in which case go straight to direction 8, below), or bear right and make your way to Kelmscott. For the latter option, follow the footpath across the fields, heading away from the river and turning sharp right to take you into the village. Bear left on to the lane and follow the lane round until you reach The Plough Inn, where you can stop for light refreshment. (A short detour up the lane on your left will take you to St George's, the 12th-century church where William Morris and his family lie buried.)

6. After a welcome break, follow the lane round to the right (keeping the pub on your right), forking left at the junction. Continue down the lane, following the signs for Kelmscott Manor. Along the way, look out for the Morris Memorial Cottages (designed by Philip Webb in 1902), on the side of which sits the famous stone carving depicting William Morris sitting beneath a tree. Kelmscott Manor, William Morris's much-loved country home, is further down the lane on the right, a mere 200m (220yd) from the river (see special feature, opposite).

7. Carry on down the lane as it bears left and then right, and at the next bend continue straight ahead along the footpath. Head across the meadow towards the river and turn right along the Thames Path to take you back to the Eaton footbridge (point 5 on the map).

8. Continue following the Thames Path as it twists and turns along the river bank. Somewhere along the way you will pass the site of another flash weir, known as Farmer's Weir. It was removed in the middle of the 18th century and the exact position is not known. You will also pass more modern – and more visible – relics, namely, two lines of World War II bunkers. They were designed as part of a last line of defence for London and the Midlands against invasion from the south, and represent only a few of the thousands that were built at the beginning of the war.

9. Follow the path over the footbridge towards Buscot Lock, where you leave the Thames Path behind you. Cross over the lock (the smallest lock on the river Thames, built in 1790) and head towards the village, crossing over the weir and bearing left on to the track. You now have the option of carrying straight on to the car park or making a short detour to St Mary's Church, where you will find a stunning set of Burne-Jones stained glass windows, a zigzag carved chancel arch, an ancient font, a Tudor arched porch, and several monuments of the Loveden family.

10. To reach the church, bear right along the marked path, passing behind the gardens of Lock Farm and crossing the field to the fine lych gate, which was erected in celebration of Queen Victoria's Diamond Jubilee in 1897. After viewing the church, retrace your steps back to the car park.

Courtesy of the Environment Agency. For more information go to www.visitthames.co.uk

A RURAL RETREAT

Built around 1600 and now Grade 1 listed, Kelmscott Manor served as William Morris's summer residence from 1871 until his death in 1896. To begin with, Morris rented the house jointly with his friend Dante Gabriel Rossetti, who used it as a discrete hideaway where he could pursue his affair with Morris's wife, Jane, while Morris was away travelling in Iceland. The house and its rural surroundings came to epitomize Morris's love of old buildings and nature, and inspired much of his work. The house, for example, is the model for 'the old house by the Thames' that features in Morris's Utopian novel *News from Nowhere* (1890), while the trees that line the Willow Walk can be found in many of Morris's designs, such as his famous Willow Boughs wallpaper. The house is only open on certain days, so check the website at www.kelmscottmanor.org.uk if you intend to visit.

Lakeland Walk

COTSWOLD WATER PARK

*Set beside the Thames on the Wiltshire/Gloucestershire border,
this fascinating walk takes you on an exploration of the Cotswold
Water Park, an area of 104km² (40 sq miles) with 140 lakes that
provide a haven for wildlife in both summer and winter. Your route
starts out following the Thames Path as it weaves its way around
some of the lakes, then heads north-west along an abandoned
railway line, before heading across farmland on the return journey.
A shortcut provides a good circular route for buggies, although parts
of this path can be flooded and very muddy all year round after wet
weather. An alternative route (see page 87) has been provided for
when the Thames Path is impassable due to flooding.*

DISTANCE:	8km (5 miles) (circular) or shorter route of 7km (4½ miles)
TIME:	Allow 2½–3 hours (2–2½ hours for shorter route)
LEVEL:	Easy, but can be very muddy after rain
START/PARKING:	Waterhay car park, beside Cleveland Lakes, south east of Ashton Keynes (nearby post code: SN6 6QY). OS grid reference SU060933 (OS Explorer map 169)
GETTING THERE:	*By car:* Exit M4 at junction 15 on to A419 to Cirencester; 4.5km (3 miles) north of Cricklade, at Spine Road Junction, take B4696 to Ashton Keynes *By public transport:* See www.traveline.org.uk for details
REFRESHMENTS:	Gateway Centre in Cotswold Water Park or The Red Lion, Cricklade
LOCAL ATTRACTIONS:	Cotswold Water Park Gateway Centre; Cotswold Country Park and Beach

DIRECTIONS

1. From the car park take the footpath near the noticeboard. Go straight on for about 50m (55yd), then turn right, following the route of the Thames Path. Continue along this path, taking note of the bird hide on the left through the gap in the hedgerow, and turning left and right as the path wends its way between the lakes. Wildlife to look out for along the way includes the Cetti's warbler, reed bunting and hobby, plus dragonflies and butterflies. After about 0.8km (½ mile) you come to a wooden gate. Go through and carry on until you reach a sharp bend.

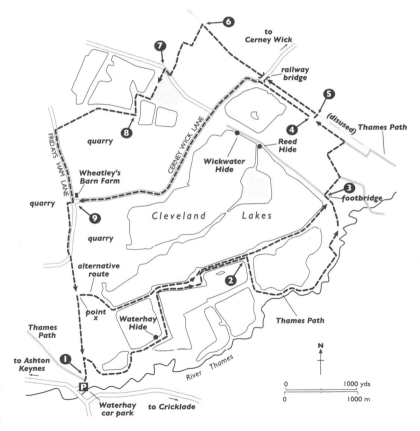

2. Follow the path as it turns right and then bears left, with the River Thames visible on your right. Continue past the green hut, ignoring the access road marked 'private road'. After about 0.5km (⅓ mile) along a tree-lined route, turn right across a narrow bridge near the interpretation panel for Cleveland Lakes. (From here you can access two bird hides through the gate as marked.)

3. Continue along the Thames Path, climbing over a low wooden stile and turning left where the path splits. At the next junction turn left and follow the signpost to South Cerney, leaving the Thames Path behind. Carry on along the path for 300m (330yd) until you reach another junction.

4. At this point you have a choice of route. For the shorter, buggy-friendly route, carry straight ahead along the track until you reach the road (Cerney Wick Lane) by the railway bridge. Turn left and continue along this road (ignoring the right turn) for about 0.8km (½ mile) until you come to a T-junction beside Wheatley's Barn Farm. Keeping a careful look out for traffic, cross over the main road (Fridays Ham Lane) next to the quarry access road opposite, where you rejoin the longer walk at point 9 on the map. For the longer route turn right here and then left, to join the old railway track at point 5.

A Haven for Wildlife – Past and Present

Covering 104km² (40 sq miles) and containing 140 lakes formed as a result of gravel extraction, the Cotswold Water Park is bigger even than the Norfolk Broads. The park is nationally important for its wintering waterbirds, with 20,000 waterfowl, comprising over 40 different species – including smew, goosander and bittern – visiting the lakes every year. In summer up to 30 breeding pairs of nightingales return to one particular site, and the area supports 23 species of dragonfly, out of a UK total of 40 species. Bats, too, are prolific, with 14 out of 17 UK species found in the area. Successful mink-trapping is helping the water-vole population to recover, and beavers are being introduced on the Lower Mill Estate. One of only two mammoth skulls ever to be found in the UK was also uncovered here, and is now on display in the Gateway Centre – well worth a visit.

5. Follow the railway track under the bridge and, after about 0.5km (⅓ mile), look for a signpost on the left to Ashton Keynes (marked 2 miles). Go over the footbridge and into the field.

6. Keeping the hedgerow on your left, walk all the way round the field edge until you reach a stile in the hedge, next to a metal gate. Go over the stile, keeping right along the edge of the field until you reach another stile set among some trees. Exit on to the road and turn right. After 40m (44yd) look out for a stile set down in the hedgerow on the left.

7. Go over the stile and follow the path straight ahead to another stile at the field edge. Go over and turn right to follow the narrow path, which can be overgrown in summer. Ignore the first gateway and follow the route of the new single-bar fence for about 0.5km (⅓ mile), passing the lake on your right.

8. Emerge on to a footbridge over a small stream and, turning right, walk round the edge of the quarry. At the end of the path turn left along verge of Fridays Ham Lane (taking great care) and walk down towards Wheatley's Barn Farm. Just before the junction with Cerney Wick Lane, cross over to the roadway next to the quarry access road.

9. Take the footpath on the left just past the private drive and follow the path as it runs parallel with the road. Where the road bears right, carefully cross over to a wooden gate and continue straight ahead along the bridlepath to make your way back to Waterhay car park.

Wet weather/flooding alternative route

If there has been a period of heavy rain, and if Waterhay car park is flooded, it means that some sections of the Thames Path will be impassable. In this case you can take an alternative route by heading up the bridleway from point 1 on the map towards point X, and turning right along the path that runs along the southern shore of the Cleveland Lakes. This path is suitable for buggies, bikes and wheelchairs, and can provide direct access to the two bird hides situated at the eastern end of the lake.

Courtesy of the Cotswold Water Park Society. For more information go to www.waterpark.org

In Search of the Source of the Thames

SAPPERTON TUNNEL, EWEN AND COATES

*This walk starts out from the southern end of Sapperton Tunnel –
once the longest tunnel in England, completed in 1789 to carry the
Thames and Severn Canal towards Cirencester and beyond. From
here you follow the disused canal for a short distance, in search of
the source of the Thames, before linking up with the Thames Path
and seeking out the infant river, which in dry weather leaves
only a grassy depression to show where it has been. As the river
gains in strength, you leave the Thames Path behind and
head off along small country lanes towards the village of
Coates and your starting point.*

DISTANCE:	10km (6½ miles) (circular)
TIME:	3–4 hours
LEVEL:	Easy
START/PARKING:	Coates Portal of Sapperton Tunnel, near Coates village. Park near The Tunnel House Inn (GL7 6PW). OS ref SO966006 (OS Explorer map 168)
GETTING THERE:	*By car:* Turn off A419 Cirencester/Stroud road to Coates and follow road to Tarlton, turning right after railway bridge to The Tunnel House Inn *By public transport:* Train to Kemble, then short walk along A429 to pick up route at direction 7
REFRESHMENTS:	The Tunnel House Inn
LOCAL ATTRACTIONS:	Rodmarton Manor

DIRECTIONS

1. Walk down the slope to the tunnel entrance and head away from the tunnel along King's Reach towards Tarlton Bridge. The concrete channel of the canal was created at the start of the 1900s in an effort to make the canal watertight, but the attempt was unsuccessful and in 1927 most of the Thames and Severn Canal was abandoned. Today, the canal is dry in summer but in winter large springs in the tunnel fill the canal with crystal-clear spring water.

2. Pass under the bridge following the towpath past the shell of Coates Round House and under the skew railway bridge. The towpath now follows a very overgrown route until you reach Trewsbury humpback bridge and the start of private ownership of the canal and towpath.

3. Follow the path up on to the bridge, turn right and walk down the track to continue along the fields. The canal is not far away to the left, hidden by undergrowth. The ground on the uphill side of the canal is the Iron Age Trewsbury Fort. In more recent times the edge of the fort became Coatesfield Quarry. The footpath follows the edges of the field, known as Trewsbury

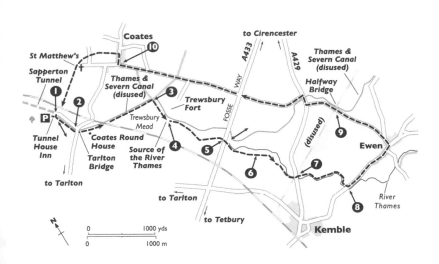

Mead, and after about 300m (330yd) an inscribed granite block comes into view in the shade of an ash tree. At the base of the tree is a small depression in the ground marking the site of a spring, believed to be the source of the River Thames (see special feature, opposite).

4. In the summer months, and sometimes in the winter, there is not a drop of water to be seen. If the winter is wet and long, however, the whole of this Cotswold valley floods and the area below the ash tree is alive with the sound of water gushing out of the ground. Flood waters permitting, continue along the bottom of the valley and up the wooden steps over the dry-stone wall. Continue to follow the Thames Path until you reach the field gate leading on to the A433 Cirencester to Tetbury road.

5. Cross this fast road with care and go down the steps into the field opposite. The line of the canal here is on the embankment to your left. The River Thames may or may not be flowing across this field, but the grassy depression shows where it should be. Cross the field by heading towards the spire of Kemble church and then gradually swing to the left to follow the edge of the field.

6. Enter the next field and note the first signs of permanent water in the river. There are several shallow depressions here that are a source of water to the river. Follow the river, which is more like a linear watercress bed, and cross the wooden footbridge over an occasional stream. The wooden slope in front of you is the embankment that is all that remains of the Great Western Railway branch line from Kemble to Cirencester. The river now flows under what was once a three-tier crossing of river, road and railway.

7. Cross the road with care and follow the Thames Path alongside the infant Thames. Each step along the footpath now seems to bring more flow into the growing river as it pushes its way through the ever-present watercress.

8. When you reach the road, turn left towards Ewen and after 100m (110yd) turn left again, forking left at the next junction. After about 0.8km (½ mile), as you approach the GWR line, look out for a track disappearing into the trees on your right.

9. If you follow this track it will soon bring you to the restored Halfway Bridge over the canal, so named because it lies halfway between Wallbridge in Stroud and Inglesham on the navigable Thames. Retrace your steps back to the lane and carry on to the A429 Kemble road. Turn right and then left towards Coates and follow the lane for 2.5km (1½ miles), crossing the A433 with care.

10. In Coates village turn right and follow the lane until you reach a footpath on the left leading to St Matthew's Church. At the rear of the churchyard turn left on to a path that takes you over the railway line and back to Sapperton Tunnel.

Courtesy of the Cotswold Canals Trust. For more information visit www.cotswoldcanals.com

A SOURCE OF DISPUTE

The granite block in Trewsbury Mead that marks the site of a spring reads: 'The Conservators of the River Thames 1857–1974: this stone was placed here to mark the source of the River Thames'. However, this is not the only place in Gloucestershire to make this claim. Another stone 17.5km (11 miles) to the north is inscribed: 'Here, O Father Thames, is your Sevenfold Spring'. The fact is, the source of the Thames is in dispute, with authorities such as the Environment Agency and Ordnance Survey placing it in Trewsbury Mead, while some claim the true source is at Seven Springs (east of Gloucester), which give rise to the River Churn – a tributary of the Thames that joins at Cricklade. Others, such as the Cotswold Canals Trust, believe the source to be springs inside the Sapperton Tunnel.

Useful Contacts

Buckinghamshire County Council
County Hall
Walton Street
Aylesbury
Buckinghamshire
HP20 1UA
tel: 0845 3708090
email: customerservices@
buckscc.gov.uk
www.buckscc.gov.uk

Chilterns AONB
Chilterns Conservation Board
The Lodge
Station Road
Chinnor
Oxon
OX39 4HA
tel: 01844 355500
email: office@chilternsaonb.org
www.chilternsaonb.org

The Countryside Agency
tel: 01242 521381
www.countryside.gov.uk
*(For more details regarding public rights
of way see: Out in the Country – Where
you can go and what you can do)*

Environment Agency
tel: 08708 506506
email: enquiries@environment-
agency.gov.uk
www.environment-
agency.gov.uk/homeandleisure

North Wessex Downs
North Wessex Downs AONB Office
Denford Manor
Hungerford
Berkshire
RG17 0UN
tel: 01488 685440
email: info@northwessex
downs.org.uk
www.northwessexdowns.org.uk

**Ridgeway/Thames Path
National Trail**
National Trails Office
Signal Court
Old Station Way
Eynsham
Oxford
OX29 4TL
tel: 01865 810224
email: ridgeway@oxfordshire.gov.uk,
Thames.Path@oxfordshire.gov.uk or
nationaltrails@naturalengland.org.uk
www.nationaltrail.co.uk/ridgeway

**Royal Borough of Windsor
and Maidenhead**
Town Hall
St Ives Road
Maidenhead
Berkshire
SL6 1RF
tel: 01628 683800
email: customer.service@rbwm.gov.uk
www.rbwm.gov.uk

Runnymede Borough Council
Runnymede Civic Centre
Station Road
Addlestone
Surrey
KT15 2AH
tel: 01932 838383
email: leisure@runnymede.gov.uk
www.runnymede.gov.uk

WILDLIFE

Berkshire, Buckinghamshire and Oxfordshire Wildlife Trust
The Lodge
1 Armstrong Road
Littlemore
Oxford
OX4 4XT
tel: 01865 775476
email: info@bbowt.org.uk
www.bbowt.org.uk

Herts & Middlesex Wildlife Trust
Grebe House
St Michael's Street
St Albans
Herts
AL3 4SN
tel: 01727 858901
email: info@hmwt.org
www.hertswildlifetrust.org.uk

RSPB (Royal Society for the Protection of Birds)
www.rspb.org.uk
(As this is a charity, to save time and money, please try to answer queries using the online search facility before emailing via online contact form; if urgent, call 01767 693680 for membership enquiries or 01767 693690 for bird and wildlife advice.)

Wiltshire Wildlife Trust
Elm Tree Court
Long Street
Devizes
Wiltshire
SN10 1NJ
tel: 01380 725670
email: see online contact form
www.wiltshirewildlife.org

WWT (Wildfowl and Wetlands Trust)
Slimbridge
Gloucestershire
GL2 7BT
tel: 01453 891900 (press 9 for a list of options)
email: enquiries@wwt.org.uk
www.wwt.org.uk

HERITAGE ORGANIZATIONS

English Heritage
29 Queen Square
Bristol
BS1 4ND
tel: 0870 333 1181
email: southeast@english-
heritage.org.uk
www.english-heritage.org.uk

Natural England
7th Floor, Hercules House
Hercules Road
London
SE1 7DU
tel: 0300 060 4911
email: enquiries@natural
england.org.uk
www.naturalengland.org.uk

The National Trust
PO Box 39
Warrington
WA5 7WD
tel: 0844 800 1895
email: enquiries@nationaltrust.org.uk
www.nationaltrust.org.uk

TRAVEL ADVICE

By car: go to the AA's Route Planner at
www.theaa.com, under 'Travel and Leisure'

By bus: go to Traveline at www.traveline.org.uk
(0871 200 2233) or Travel Search at www.carlberry.co.uk

By train: go to National Rail Enquiries at
www.nationalrail.co.uk (08457 48 49 50)